Essential
Mainland
Greece

by
MIKE GERRARD

Mike Gerrard is a freelance writer who has bee
visiting Greece for more than 20 years. He contributes
regularly to the travel pages of newspapers and
magazines.

AA

Produced by AA Publishing

**Written by Mike Gerrard
Peace and Quiet section
by Paul Sterry
Original photography by
Richard Surman**

Edited, designed and produced
by AA Publishing. Maps ©
The Automobile Association 1994

Distributed in the United Kingdom
by AA Publishing, Fanum House,
Basingstoke, Hampshire,
RG21 2EA.

The contents of this publication
are believed correct at the time of
printing. Nevertheless, the
publishers cannot be held
responsible for any errors or
omissions, or for changes in
details given in this guide or for
the consequences of any reliance
on the information provided by
the same. Assessments of
attractions, hotels, restaurants and
so forth are based upon the
author's own experience and,
therefore, descriptions given in
this guide necessarily contain an
element of subjective opinion
which may not reflect the
publisher's opinion or dictate a
reader's own experience on
another occasion.
**We have tried to ensure
accuracy in this guide, but
things do change and we would
be grateful if readers would
advise us of any inaccuracies
they may encounter.**

A CIP catalogue record for this
book is available from the British
Library.

ISBN 0 7495 0712 8

Published by AA Publishing,
which is a trading name of
Automobile Association
Developments Limited, whose
registered office is Fanum House,
Basingstoke, Hampshire,
RG21 2EA.
Registered number 1878835.

Colour separation: BTB Colour
Reproduction Ltd, Whitchurch,
Hampshire

Printed by: Printers Trento S.R.L.,
Italy

Front cover picture: The Parthenon

A note on Greek place-names
There are often several alternative versions when Greek place-names are
transcribed into the Roman alphabet. In headings of place descriptions,
and in the Index, this book uses the version corresponding with AA maps,
but more familiar anglicised spellings (given in brackets in the headings)
are sometimes used in the text.

Contents

This book employs a simple rating system to help choose which places to visit:

 'top ten'

 ◆◆◆ do not miss
◆◆ see if you can
◆ worth seeing if you have time

Introduction and Background

INTRODUCTION

To encounter Greek hospitality for the first time can be overwhelming to visitors from countries where strangers tend to be treated with suspicion. To the Greeks, a stranger is a guest. They even have a word for it – *xenos* – just one word, since in Greece a stranger *is* a guest. Greek hospitality manifests itself in a variety of ways: a gift of a flower when you are passing someone's garden, a drink freely bought, a cigarette offered, a bunch of grapes given or even an entire meal shared, after which your Greek host may be insulted if you insist on trying to pay. Of course, such generosity should soon start to work both ways, as the visitor, inevitably, begins to wonder why we can't all be more like the Greeks. But the Greeks are unique.

This is not to say that you will not also occasionally encounter a less than generous attitude. The prospect of prosperity from tourism can bring greed. Greece is no exception, but it may help to remember the old wisecrack that 90 per cent of Greek people are honest and helpful, and the rest go to Athens and become taxi-drivers.

You are likely to find the legendary hospitality even more in evidence on the Greek mainland than on the overcrowded islands. Mainland Greece also offers much more varied scenery than the more popular islands. Beach-lovers need not sacrifice their sun-worship: the country's small size and irregular shape mean

One of many familiar images of Greece today. Soldiers representing different regiments of the Greek army take turns to guard the **Vouli** *(Parliament building) and the Memorial to the Unknown Soldier in Athens*

Detail of an Ionic column at Delfi

that it is impossible to be more than a few hours' drive from the coast. And what coasts they are – from bustling Khalkhidiki and popular Parga to the sweeping, dramatic and uncrowded seaboards of the Pilion (Pelion) peninsula or the Mani.

Greece has some of the most spectacular scenery in the southern Mediterranean – and a climate to match, with sunshine from April to October. Everyone has heard of Crete's Samaria Gorge – the longest in Europe – but few know the Vikos Gorge in northwest Greece, the second longest and considered by many to be more spectacular, with walls almost 1000m high. Around it are the Pindhos (Pindus) mountains, rising to 2500m, while on the Pilion peninsula it is possible to lose yourself amid a heavily forested landscape.

Naturally Greece is known for its classical sites – among the greatest in the world, alongside those of Egypt, Peru, Mexico or Italy. Who could fail to be excited at seeing the home of the Greek gods on Mount Olimbos (Olympos); the site of the oracle of Delfi; or the original running track still in existence at Olimbia (Olympia), birthplace of the Olympic Games and the place where the Olympic torch, uniting the whole world, is still lit?

Reminders of Ancient Greece may abound, but the country today is a very special blend of ancient and modern. The contrasts are everywhere. On beaches girls in skimpy bikinis will be sunbathing while close by unshaven fishermen mend their nets as Greek fishermen have done for the last few thousand years. In Athens the 2,500-year-old classical ruins on the Akropolis still stand magnificent and proud, as if passing silent judgement on the cacophony of traffic in the streets below. A black-clad priest, the *papas*, emerges from worship in the gloom of a candle-lit Byzantine church and stops at the neon-lit supermarket to buy a packet of cigarettes. Greece absorbs the new without losing the old.

Greece absorbs visitors readily too. A steady increase in tourism since the 1960s had made Greece one of Europe's most popular holiday destinations by the 1980s. Facilities have improved so that few towns are without a

Icons are to be seen almost anywhere in Greece: in homes and wayside shrines, as well as in churches and chapels. This one is in the Byzantine Museum in Athens

range of hotels and restaurants. Most still have a unique Greek approach, though. The hot water in your bathroom may come out of the cold tap (the eccentricities of Greek plumbing are legendary), the wardrobe door may not open unless you rearrange the furniture, and even in the smartest restaurant you may find yourself escorted into the kitchen to see what is cooking on the stove. Greek menus do not go in for elaborate descriptions. It is much easier to let the guest choose by the look and the smell of each dish.

The Greek approach to life is very relaxed. Time is flexible: in rural areas the local bus may leave 15 minutes early, or 30 minutes late, depending on whether the driver has to pick up his cousin or deliver a package to a friend on the way. Never expect to be able to make an exact appointment: 'this afternoon' or 'this evening' will usually be close enough.

For the Greeks there are more important matters than time – things such as hospitality, honesty, conversation and enjoying life. These qualities soon rub off on the visitor – the guest who is very unlikely to be a stranger for long.

BACKGROUND

The Greeks are a patriotic people, sure of their national identity and of what it means to be Greek – for better or worse. They are a people in touch with the past. Visitors need to be aware of this, not just in order to have a greater understanding of classical sites but also in order to know something of the present way of life in Greece, and to appreciate where the visitor fits in.

Athens and the hill of Likavitos, seen from the Akropolis. The view is not always as clear as this: Athens in summer is notorious for its pollution-induced smog

Greece Today

Greece is not a rich country. It welcomes the money generated by tourism. Many a poor fishing community has been transformed by turning itself into a tourist resort. This may be decried by those visitors who prefer 'their' villages 'unspoilt', but it is unrealistic to expect them to remain undisturbed for much of the year so that a select few visitors can enjoy

Greek village life for the holiday season. The first families in a village to cater for tourists can become wealthy by local standards – a rare opportunity of a higher standard of living in coastal areas where fishing stocks have

MAINLAND GREECE

*Below right:
Tourism in the
'90s. The
prosperous can be
pampered at the
Astir Palace, one of
the top luxury
hotels in Athens*

become depleted as populations rise.
Greek people love their country, but this does
not necessarily extend to keeping it tidy. Many
of them would see nothing ironic in admiring
the view while tossing an empty cigarette
packet over their shoulder (the Greeks smoke
like the chimneys on their ferries). Rubbish tips
often seem to be sited in the most picturesque

Opposite: The restored classical theatre at Dhodhoni, near Ioannina

Ethnic fare to take home: olive oil, pistachio nuts, figs and olives – not forgetting the ouzo, retsina and Metaxa brandy

spots. Be warned, however, that visitors are not expected to treat the surroundings with equal disdain. Greece is like a family whose members can criticise each other, but take a dim view of outsiders who dare to do the same.

Family and village life is at the heart of Greece. You will often see an old man or woman walking hand in hand with a toddling grandchild. Friends will walk arm in arm, too. In many places the evening stroll, known as the *volta*, has become a tradition. Here families and friends in Sunday best walk up and down the same route, usually the seafront or town square, on the same night each week, greeting each other. In some places the *volta* is a nightly routine. This is a chance, too, for the young men and women of the village to catch each other's eye, and perhaps to arrange a secret rendezvous.

The affairs of the young are still strictly controlled, mainly to protect the women. While it might be accepted for a young man to sow his wild oats with a succession of female tourists, a young girl is expected to preserve her virtue for her future husband.

Visitors, too, should be aware of the need for modesty on occasion. For visits to churches or monasteries, men should wear trousers rather than shorts, while women should wear a skirt of a decent length and a top with sleeves that at least cover the shoulders. In many places this code of dress will be ignored in practice, but in a particularly holy place, such as Meteora, a visitor wearing shorts may well be turned away at the door.

Discretion is also called for when sunbathing. In many places topless sunbathing is common, but it may not be appreciated on a family beach in the middle of a town. Use your own judgement. Nude sunbathing is technically illegal, but is frequently encountered on out-of-the-way beaches. No one minds too much, as long as you are discreet.

Religion

Family life in Greece centres round the church, which is Greek Orthodox. Sunday morning services are usually well attended, and visitors

will be welcome. The services are much less formal affairs than one might expect from the strong religious beliefs that prevail. As the services are long, some people go just for part of the service and then leave again, having a quiet chat with friends on the way. This is a typical example of the unique Greek mixture of formality and informality, which can leave foreign visitors rather bemused as to how to behave.

The same mixture applies to the life of the priest, who is much more a part of the community than in many other countries. In his black garb, hair tucked under his stovepipe hat, he will often be seen sitting in a café, enjoying a smoke and a coffee with the other men. This does not mean, though, that he is not treated with great reverence.

Zagoria, high in the Pindhos mountains near the Albanian border, is an area in which to discover the scenery and wildlife of Greece at their unspoilt best

*Markets change
little with the years*

Easter is a particularly good time to visit
Greece if you wish to see a true celebration of
religious beliefs. This is the most important
time of the Greek year, when a period of
fasting is followed by great joy and celebration
(see **Special Events**, page 106–7). Again,
strangers are likely to be made most welcome.

Historic Greece

Many visitors to Greece probably have little
interest in its grand history, as long as the sun
shines and the people are friendly. But then,
most visitors go to the islands. The average
visitor to the Greek mainland is likely to want to
look at sites such as the Akropolis, Delfi or
Olympia, where a little background knowledge
helps. Likewise, some grasp of the story of
Greece in more recent times sheds light on
many aspects of the country today – from
architecture to politics.

Early Civilisations

The very earliest archaeological finds in
Greece go back to Palaeolithic times, but the
first civilisation to have made its mark with a
significant legacy of fine artefacts was based in
the Cyclades in the 3rd millennium BC.
Archaeologists think that these seafaring
Cycladic people had some contact with the
beginnings of a very sophisticated culture in
Crete – that of the Minoans, centred on
Knossos, and existing from roughly 2000BC to
1400BC.
At about the time that the Minoans mysteriously
disappeared – possibly wiped out by tidal
wave or invading forces – other societies were
developing on the mainland. The most
prominent – all in the Peloponnese – were at
Tiryns, near Navplion; near Pilos, where the
remains of Nestor's Palace can still be seen;
and at Mikinai (Mycenae), whose glorious
golden treasures are on display in Athens.

Classical and Makedhonian Greece

At that time Athens was only one of several
important city-states. Like its long-standing
rival, Sparta, it had rejected oligarchy – the
autocratic system of government favoured by
most of the other city-states – in favour of a new

Cistus is a common plant on sunny hillsides. Abundant wild flowers are one of the joys of Greece in spring and early summer

system, democracy, where citizens (but not women, foreigners or slaves) participated in government. Each city-state clung fiercely to its chosen system of government, and to its autonomy.

By the 5th century BC, disagreements between Athens and Sparta over the balance of power between them erupted into the Peloponnesian War, which divided the Greek world for some 30 years. Ironically, this strife-torn time was during the so-called Classical period – Greece's Golden Age, during which the arts flourished and Greece's status as the cradle of civilisation became firmly established. The philosopher Socrates, and later his pupil Plato and the influential thinker Aristotle were teaching in Athens. Like them, great classical writers, from Herodotus and Thucydides the historians, to Aeschylus and Euripedes the dramatists, were producing work that would still be studied 2,500 years later. The Parthenon was built, the Battle of Marathon took place, the Oracle at Delfi was being consulted

Elevsis today is a far cry from the 'Elysian Fields' of Classical Greece. In the 5th century BC this was one of the most important sanctuaries of the ancient world

and the Olympic Games were flourishing. These are times you will come across again and again on your travels.

At the end of the Classical period came the Makedhonian age. Philip of Makedhonia came to power in 359BC, and conquered much of the Greek mainland in his attempt to unite the scattered city-states. In 336BC he was succeeded by his son, Alexander the Great. One of Alexander's tutors had been Aristotle, who went on to found a school in Athens. The young, ambitious and frighteningly efficient Alexander wanted to unite not only the Greek states, but the whole known world – under his rule, of course. He conquered Persia and the Middle East, and was looking to invade Arabia when he finally died, in Babylon, in 323BC – aged only 33.

Rome, Byzantium and the Ottoman Empire
Greek life and culture continued to flourish until Greece fell to the Roman Empire in 205BC. There followed 500 years of Roman rule –

BACKGROUND

Landscape near the Prespa Lakes in northwestern Greece. Life in remote and rural corners such as this has escaped the radical changes that have transformed the cities and coasts in recent decades

hence the Roman ruins in Athens and elsewhere. As the Romans eventually declined in power to the west, so the Emperor Constantine took over the eastern part of the former Roman Empire, making his capital the city of Byzantium, which became Constantinople, now Istanbul. With the rising sun of Byzantium in the east, Athens fell from prominence, and for many centuries Greece remained something of a backwater.

The Byzantine age lasted for almost 1,000 years, from the 5th to the 15th centuries AD, though during the later part of this period the Venetians were ruling parts of Greece, and the Ottoman Turks were casting an ever more threatening shadow across the Byzantine world. There followed the dark days of the Turkish Occupation, from 1453 to 1821. The conflict between Christianity and Islam touched much of Eastern Europe during this time. Greece, at the heart of the region, was ruled by Turks – ruthless occupiers alien in both language and religion. Greek culture and language relied for their survival during this period on the Greek Orthodox Church, especially in those of its many monasteries that were tucked away in remote, mountainous areas.

From Independence to Civil War

The dawn of a new era for Greece had its beginnings on 25 March 1821 – the day the Greek War of Independence began, near Kalavrita. Many classically educated foreigners espoused the Greek cause, and some (including, most famously, the British poet Lord Byron) took up arms for Greece. Ships from Britain, France and Russia were instrumental in the decisive Turkish defeat at the Battle of Navarino in 1827, but it was not until 1832 that these foreign governments reached agreement among themselves which allowed Greece to be proclaimed an independent kingdom.

Independence was slow to bring prosperity, and many Greeks remained dissatisfied with the new political arrangements. Foreign powers continued to intervene – not least by appointing Greece's monarch – and government from Athens was often resented in

St George's Chapel at Vravrona (Brauron) dates from the 15th century – the closing years of the Byzantine period. Byzantine architecture can be seen in many Greek churches and chapels

The mountain village of Arakhova, near Delfi

the fiercely independent regions. The country's long history of conflict continued. During World War II, after notorious provocation by Mussolini,Greece was invaded again, only to have the occupying German army replaced by a bloody civil war which lasted until 1949.

From the Colonels to PASOK
The military junta of the Greek Colonels was imposed quite unexpectedly in Athens one night in April 1967. All traces of democracy – born in the same city almost 2,500 years earlier – were banished. Martial law, strict censorship of the press and the sacking of many civil servants and others suspected of left-wing sympathies were among a host of

repressive measures introduced. Eventually, after the junta's ineptitude had led to economic chaos and had provoked the Turks into invading Cyprus, the Colonels were ousted in the summer of 1974, and elections restored. The PASOK socialist party and the right-wing New Democracy party have vied for power since then, each taking a turn in government, though seldom commanding a significant majority. Greece became a member of the European Community in 1981 – another issue that divided the nation. Greece's politics, like its people, is a matter of extremes and contradictions.

Rural Greece still clings tenaciously to its old ways. Mules and donkeys are often to be seen carrying people or goods (and frequently both at once)

The State, the People and the EC

Greece, to the Greeks, is *Hellas*, and for official purposes it is the Hellenic Republic. About one-third of its 11-million population are farmers, and another third live in and around Athens. Fishing and tourism account for many of the rest, and in addition to the income generated by foreign visitors, the economy relies on money sent home by Greeks who live abroad. There are approximately 5 million of these, particularly in America and Australia: Melbourne has more Greek residents than any city outside Athens.

Greece remains one of the EC's poorest members. It received substantial loans from the Community in the mid-1980s, and the accompanying austerity measures helped stabilise its inflationary economy. Such measures were recently reinforced, and you will hear many Greeks complaining about high taxes and low wages – despite the fact that an estimated one-third of the population escape the tax system. A recent government amnesty on past tax misdemeanours was a dismal failure; few people elected to become tax-payers. Many Greeks regard the avoidance of taxes – and indeed of any laws with which they disagree – as a matter of principle, so it is not surprising that membership of the EC has probably had less effect on the average Greek than on any other European citizen. Attempts to impose EC regulations have had little effect on Greece and her resolutely independent people.

What to See

The Essential rating system:

✓	'top ten'

◆◆◆   do not miss
◆◆   see if you can
◆   worth seeing if you
        have time

Greece covers some 130,000sq km. This land area includes 6,000 islands, about 200 of which are inhabited. The mainland forms the southern end of Europe's Balkan peninsula.

Much of the land is mountainous, the highest peak being the mythical home of the ancient Greek Gods, Olimbos (Olympos), at 2917m. There are several other mountains almost as high, and magnificent ranges such as Parnassos, north of Delfi, the Pindhos (Pindus) mountains, close to the Albanian border, and the dramatic and dangerous Taiyetos (Taygettus) range in the southern Peloponnese. To be almost constantly in sight of mountains or sea, and frequently both, makes Greece one of Europe's most scenically beautiful countries.

Mainland Greece has more than enough 'sights' – classical ruins, museums and historic towns – to fill any holiday. Inevitably, details of such places make up many of the descriptions on the following

Meteora: a fairytale landscape

pages. But seasoned travellers to Greece will know that a truer feeling for the country will be gained by unexpected discoveries of lesser-known villages and landscapes. Mainland Greece offers plenty of scope for this kind of exploration: there are almost limitless opportunities off the beaten track.

For the purposes of this book, the Greek mainland has been divided into five main areas. **Athinai (Athens)** deserves a section to itself, of course, and another – **Around Athens** – has been given to places of interest most easily reached from the capital. **Peloponnisos (The Peloponnese)** is the most southerly portion of mainland Greece, and technically became an island in 1893, when the Corinth Canal severed it from the rest of Greece. **Thessaloniki and the North** brings together the large administrative regions of Makedhonia (Macedonia) and Thraki (Thrace), leaving the rest of the mainland conveniently grouped together under the heading of **Central Greece**.

ATHÍNAI (ATHENS)

Greece is the cradle of European civilisation, and Athens its capital. To do the city justice requires much longer than a fleeting weekend visit.

A city is about its inhabitants as much as its monuments, and people-watching in Greece is always a rewarding activity. Find time to sit in the cafés on Platia Sindagma (Syntagma Square), or take a leisurely lunch in a taverna, and watch the world go by. Visit the flea-market of Monastiraki and the nearby bazaar area, not just the souvenir shops in the Plaka. The drawback to strolling round Athens is the terrible traffic pollution, and the resulting smog cloud often visible from the heights of the Akropolis or Likavitos (Lykabettos) hill. A visit to one of the many coffee-houses or lesser-known tourist attractions can be a welcome relief from the crowds, the heat and the fumes.

Some of Athens' smaller museums are a true delight, and it would be a shame to visit the city and not have time to take in the specialist Goulandris collection of Cycladic art, or the museum devoted to Greek musical instruments. Allow time to look inside some of the hundreds of tiny Byzantine churches that are dotted about the city, and to take in sites other than the Akropolis: the Agora, for example, or the remains of the largest temple in Greece, the Olympion Dhios (Temple of Olympian Zeus). This temple was completed almost 2,000 years ago, by which time Athens had already been in existence for 3,000 years. Consider this when planning a visit.

◆◆◆

AGORÁ

reached from either Adhrianou or Theorias streets
(museum tel: 321–0185)
Close to the Akropolis, the site of the ancient Agora (market place) should not be missed. Its main attraction is its museum – not so much for the small collection it contains (though that has its own delights) as for the building itself. This was originally the **Stoa Attalou** (**Stoa of Attalos**), an arcade in the market area. It has been faithfully and magnificently restored by the efforts – and money – of the American School of Archaeology in Athens. The result is an elegant colonnaded building giving one of the few present-day impressions of the glory that was Greece. The large open space outside is rather a jumble of ruins, dominated at one end by the attractive lines of the **Temple of Hephaistos**. Known also as the **Thission**, this well-preserved Doric temple dates from the 5th century BC, serving in its time as a church and a cemetery.
Open: Tuesday to Sunday, 08.30–15.00hrs.
Closed: public holidays.
Metro: Monastiraki or Thission.

The ultimate emblem of Classical Athens – the Parthenon

roped off to prevent further damage to its features from the never-ending stream of visitors. To add to its problems, acid rain and air pollution have taken their toll on the masonry.

Like all the main buildings on the Akropolis, the Parthenon dates from the 5th century BC. It is renowned for having no straight lines in its construction – despite appearances, its columns and beams taper gently. The building originally contained a huge gold and ivory statue of the goddess Athena the Virgin ('Athena Parthenos'). Traces of iron in its marble give the Parthenon a golden glow, especially striking at sunset.

The Parthenon may be the most impressive building on the Akropolis, but there are others to see too. On the left as you enter stand the remains of the original grand entrance, the **Propylaia**. Holes in its walls indicate where support beams were placed to hold the upper floors. To the right is the **Temple of Athena Nike**, which in 1686 was completely demolished by the Turks to enable them to use its strategic position for military purposes. The temple was reassembled in the 19th century.

The other major building whose remains can still be seen on the Akropolis is the **Erechtheion**. This has a special importance for the Greeks, as it is said to be the

◆◆◆
AKROPOLIS (ACROPOLIS)
(tel: 321–0219)

This great rock, whose name means 'upper city', was the focal point of Athenian life from earliest times. Temples and public buildings had come and gone here for generations before the Golden Age of Classical Greece saw the Akropolis crowned by the buildings whose ruins survive today. For most people the huge Doric temple called the **Parthenon** is the symbol of Athens. Familiar yet awe-inspiring, to see it for the first time is like a first glimpse of the Pyramids or the Eiffel Tower. The Parthenon, like Athens in general, has suffered from the excesses of the 20th century. It is now

place where Athena brought forth the first olive tree. In the nearby **Pandroseion** grows an olive tree planted to commemorate the original. At the far end, the **Mousio**

Akropoli (Akropolis Museum; tel: 323–6665) houses a splendid collection of statues, masks, pediments and some portions of the Parthenon frieze – though you will have to travel to London to see the finest sections of the frieze. They were removed from the Akropolis by the now notorious Lord Elgin in 1803 and sold to the British Museum.

Open: site Monday to Friday 08.00–19.00hrs (16.45hrs in winter), Saturday and Sunday 08.30–14.45hrs; museum Tuesday to Friday 08.00–16.30hrs, Saturday, Sunday and holidays 08.30–14.45hrs.
Bus: 230.
Metro: Thission.

◆
ÁRIOS PÁGOS (AREOPAGOS)

Almost opposite the Akropolis entrance, stone steps carved in the rock lead to the Areopagos, where the supreme court of Athens once stood. The name means 'Hill of Mars': the legend is that here Mars, the god of war (Ares to the Greeks), was tried for murdering one of the sons of Poseidon. In AD 54 St Paul delivered his Sermon to the Athenians from the Areopagos. The text is inscribed on a bronze plaque. The site is noted more for its views than for the few ancient foundations that remain.
Open: at all times.
Metro: Monastiraki or Thission.

◆◆◆
ATHINAS/EOLOU STREETS (BAZAAR AREA)

between Monastiraki and Omonia squares
Stalls line the streets and the hubbub of open-air

The Akropolis by night

commerce is unmistakable in the bazaar area, centred on Athinas and Eolou streets. On stalls and in shops, housewives and tourists alike haggle over all manner of goods, ranging from tools and buckets to clothes and antiques. The many and various food stores offer a chance to buy bread, olives and cheese for a picnic, or spices and herbs to take home as presents. There is a Sunday morning flower market near the Platia Ayias Irinis, and a large meat and seafood market at the junction of Athinas and Evripidhou streets. The displays of fresh fish and cuts of meat, and the sheer bustle of the place (all day every day), offer a lively antidote to visiting historic sites.

◆
ETHNIKÍ PINAKOTHÍKI (NATIONAL GALLERY)
Leoforos Vasilissis Konstandinou 50 (tel: 721–1010)
This is not well signposted but is the ugly block of a building opposite the Hilton Hotel. A visit here may be disappointing by comparison with equivalent galleries in other capital cities, but there is plenty for visitors interested in the work of Greek artists, including perhaps the greatest of them all, the Cretan El Greco.
Other European artists represented include Picasso, Breughel, Rembrandt, Goya and van Dyck, but not even this small collection is permanently on display.
Open: Tuesday to Saturday 09.00–15.00hrs, Sunday 10.00–14.00hrs.
Closed: public holidays.
Bus: 234.

◆
ETHNIKO MOUSÍO (NATIONAL HISTORICAL MUSEUM)
Platia Kolokotronis, Stadiou 13 (tel: 323–7617)
A visit to this museum also offers a chance to see the impressive debating chamber of the Old Parliament Building. The collection itself will be of more interest to historians and military enthusiasts. It includes many busts and paintings, medals and war mementoes. One room has a collection of Lord Byron memorabilia, while others display folk costumes.
Open: Tuesday to Friday 09.00–13.30hrs, Saturday and Sunday 09.00–12.30hrs (free admission Thursday).
Closed: public holidays.
Bus: 1, 2, 4, 5, 11, 12.

◆◆
ETHNIKÓS KÍPOS
(NATIONAL GARDENS)
southeast of Syntagma Square; entrances behind and to south of Parliament building
Also known as the Royal Gardens, these were laid out by Queen Amalia, wife of Otho, the first king of Greece. They offer a shady and peaceful retreat from the noisy city streets, with tree-lined pathways, ponds, cafés and children's play areas. Swarms of stray cats and a sad attempt at a zoo are less pleasing features.
Open: daily, sunrise to sunset.
Bus: 2, 4, 11, 12.

◆
KENTRO ELLINIKIS
PARADOSIS
(CENTRE OF HELLENIC TRADITION)
Pandhrossou 36
Housed in an arcade off the Plaka's main shopping street, this is a good place to buy traditional Greek arts and crafts items such as embroidery, paintings and pottery. An excellent and very popular café/restaurant has window seats offering a good view down on to the passing parade outside.
Open: Tuesday and Thursday 09.00–19.00hrs, Wednesday, Friday and Saturday 09.00–13.00hrs and 17.00–21.00hrs, Sunday 09.00–13.00hrs.
Metro: Monastiraki.

◆
KENTRO LAIKIS TEXNIS KAI
PARADOSIS
(CENTRE FOR POPULAR ARTS AND TRADITIONS)
Angelikis Hatzimikali 6 (tel: 324–3987)
This tiny collection of silverware, clothing, icons, silver bibles and ornate chalices is similar in its coverage to the much bigger and better Museum of Greek Folk Art (see page 31), but admission here is free, with the bonus of a chance to see inside one of the older Plaka mansions.
Open: Tuesday and Thursday 09.00–21.00hrs, Wednesday, Friday and Saturday 09.00–13.00hrs and 17.00–21.00hrs, Sunday 09.00–13.00hrs.
Closed: public holidays.
Metro: Monastiraki.

Urban oasis: the National Gardens

Keramikos, the ancient cemetery

◆◆
KERAMIKI SILOGI APO TO MOUSIO TIS ELLINIKIS LAOGRAFIAS (CERAMIC COLLECTION OF THE MUSEUM OF GREEK FOLK ART)

Tzami Tsistarakis, Monastiraki, Areos 1 (tel: 324-2066/323–9813)
This interesting collection is housed in the Mosque of Tsistarakis, built in 1759 and used over the years as a jail and a barracks. Following earthquake damage, the mosque has been sympathetically restored and is now a bright and roomy setting for an enjoyable collection of mainly bold and primitive pottery. The work is mostly by potters who were refugees from Asia Minor, and the detailed biographical information in Greek and English tells some fascinating life stories.
Open: Wednesday to Monday, 09.00–14.30hrs.
Closed: public holidays.
Metro: Monastiraki.

◆
KERAMIKOS (KERAMEIKOS CEMETERY)

Ermou 148 (tel: 346–3552)
The principal cemetery of ancient Athens was in the Keramikos (potters') quarter of the city. Here visitors may see tombs and archaeological finds dating back to the 11th century BC. Many tombstones have been replaced as they were, some lining the grand **Street of the Tombs**, which was reserved for the rich. The museum contains good displays of the potter's art.
Open: Tuesday to Sunday, 08.30–15.00hrs, including holidays.
Bus: 025.
Metro: Thission.

◆◆◆
LIKAVITÓS (LYKABETTOS HILL)

The prospect of walking to the top of the 277m hill of Likavitos may seem daunting, and many will opt for the regular funicular service from Ploutarhou (08.00–22.00hrs), yet the climb is not steep. The path gently zig-zags through pine-scented woods, with plenty of seating for rests. A café half-way up offers drinks and snacks (at predictably inflated prices), while another at the top is popular for its evening views across to the floodlit Akropolis – perfect for a brandy after dinner. On a clear day the views stretch from the plains and hills around Athens, down to the harbour at Piraeus. Also at the top is a chapel and below it a modern open-air theatre.

◆◆
MITRÓPOLIS

Platia Mitropoleos
In Mitropolis Square are two
contrasting churches. **Megali
Mitropolis** (Great Mitropolis)
is the Cathedral of Athens,
known officially as
Evangelismos (the
Annunciation, as depicted
above the main doorway),
and unofficially as Ayios
Nikolaos, the name of the
monastery that stood here
until 1827. The modern
church was completed in
1862, is almost always open,
and is more attractive inside
than out. Dwarfed alongside it
is the more appealing 12th-
century **Mikri Mitropolis**
(Little Mitropolis), dedicated
to Ayios Eleftherios. This
church is normally closed, but
in any case the exterior is its
best feature.
Bus: 025.
Metro: Monastiraki.

◆◆◆
MONASTIRÁKI

This small square gets its
name because a monastery
once stood here. Anything
less monastic today would be
hard to imagine. This is one of
the focal points of the city,
with a busy metro station and
a host of lively cafés and
market stalls. To the west is
the Monastiraki area, where
the Plaka souvenir shops give
way to the flea-market, open
every day but packed on
Sunday mornings. Here are
second-hand books, third-
hand bric-a-brac, dusty
postcards, bouzoukis,
copperware and coins – in

short, everything from
religious icons to
pornography.
Bus: 025.
Metro: Monastiraki.

◆
MOUSÍO ATHINON
(MUSEUM OF THE CITY OF
ATHENS)

*Paparigopoulou 7 (tel:
323–0168)*
Despite being the original Royal
Palace, home of King Otho I,
this is an easily missed small
white building on the south side
of Platia Klafthomonos. The
refurbished royal apartments
are surprisingly modest, and
the walls display many prints
and paintings of Athens over
the years. The most striking
exhibit is an admirably detailed
scale model of Athens in 1842,
when there were a mere 300
houses.
Open: Monday, Wednesday,
Friday, Saturday
09.00–13.30hrs (free
admission Wednesday).
Closed: public holidays and
July.
Bus: 1, 2, 4, 5, 11, 12.

◆◆
MOUSÍO BENÁKI (BENAKI
MUSEUM)

Koumbari 1 (tel: 361–1617)
Housed in the mansion home of
the museum's founder, Antoine
Emmanuel Benaki, a cotton
trader who collected Greek and
Egyptian items, this is an
excellent small museum. The
basement has a Greek folk art
collection of ceramics,
costumes, wooden carvings
and particularly fine jewellery.
Elsewhere there are paintings
by El Greco, Lord Byron's

Great Mitropolis and its square

writing desk and a 17th-century Egyptian reception room, complete with fountain. The museum's rooftop café and tastefully stocked shop are other good reasons to visit.
Open: Wednesday to Monday 08.30–14.00hrs.
Closed: public holidays.
Bus: 023, 234.

MOUSIO ELLINIKIS LAOGRAFIAS (MUSEUM OF GREEK FOLK ART)

Kidhathinion 17 (tel: 321–3018)
The only drawback of this large collection on several floors is lack of space. One floor covers silk production, the top floor houses a collection of folk costumes, while another is devoted to the intricate work of Greek silversmiths. A small shop also has craft items for sale.
Open: Tuesday to Sunday,
10.00–16.00hrs.
Closed: public holidays.
Bus: 024, 230.

MOUSIO ELLINIKON MOUSIKON ORGANON (MUSEUM OF GREEK MUSICAL INSTRUMENTS)

Dhioyenous 1–3 (tel: 325–0198)
This delightful modern museum has three floors, each devoted to a different type of instrument. Headphones allow visitors to hear recorded examples while reading the explanations in either Greek or English. One set of photographs shows how to make music from that most basic Greek combination: worry-beads and wine-glass. An extensive collection of Greek music is on sale in the shop.
Open: Tuesday to Sunday 10.00–14.00hrs, except Wednesday 12.00–18.00hrs.
Closed: public holidays.
Metro: Monastiraki.

ATHENS

◆◆◆
MOUSÍO ETHNIKÓ ARKHEOLOGIKÓ

(NATIONAL ARCHAEOLOGICAL MUSEUM)
Patission 28 (tel: 821–7717)
Allow at least half a day here – or at least two visits if you hope to have more than a glimpse of the largest collection of Greek art in the world. Highlights include beautiful frescoes from houses on the island of Thira (Santorini), which were contemporaneous with the Cretan Minoan civilisation before being engulfed in the island's massive earthquake. An exhibition elsewhere displays treasures from Mikinai (Mycenae), including the famous gold mask discovered by Heinrich Schliemann (see pages 81–2). Many of the statues will be familiar, including a magnificent figure of Poseidon about to throw his trident, while on a more delicate scale, the *Little Jockey* shows a young boy encouraging his horse with great urgency and grace.
The museum has a separate coin collection, displaying some of its 400,000 coins. The entrance is on the first floor or from a side entrance at Tositsa 1. Here too is the Epigraphical Collection, where many historical inscriptions may be studied.
Open: Monday 11.00–17.00hrs, Tuesday to Friday 08.00–17.00hrs, Saturday, Sunday and holidays 08.30–15.00hrs.
Metro: Omonia.

National Archaeological Museum

◆◆◆
MOUSÍO GOULANDRI KIKLÁDHIKI TEXNI (GOULANDRIS MUSEUM OF CYCLADIC ART)
Neofytou Douka 4 (tel: 723–4931/724–9706)
This first-class museum was created to house the private collection of Nikolas P. Goulandris, a ship-owner and patron of the arts. The displays span many centuries of ancient Greek art, but the central items are the beautiful artefacts of the Cycladic civilisation of 3000–2000BC. The statues are especially memorable, the figures seemingly floating in the space of their display cabinets. Subtle lighting brings out their shape and texture. Be prepared to be tempted to take home a copy from the attractive museum shop.
Open: Monday and Wednesday to Friday 10.00–16.00hrs, Saturday 10.00–15.00hrs.
Closed: public holidays.
Bus: 234.

Cycladic Culture

Early maritime trade between Europe and Asia Minor brought prosperity and new ideas to Aegean islands such as Syros and Naxos. By 3,000BC a remarkable and brilliant culture was flourishing in the Cyclades, and producing exceptional works of art. Local marble was often used to make small statues whose smooth, simple lines still manage to convey great depth of feeling, and have inspired modern artists from Modigliani to Henry Moore. The function of the statues is unknown, but they are often thought to have been linked with some kind of fertility cult.

◆
MOUSÍO KANELLÓPOULOS (KANELLOPOULOS MUSEUM)

Panou/Theorias (tel: 321–2313)
This small broad-ranging collection is housed in a neo-classical Plaka mansion. It concentrates on religion and antiquity, with a number of icons from the 14th to the 17th centuries. They include some in near-perfect condition, the colours almost leaping from the woodwork. Jewellery includes a fine gold pendant from the 9th century, and a bracelet from the 11th or 12th century. There are also some lovely miniature bronzes.
Open: Tuesday to Sunday 08.30–15.00hrs.
Bus: 025.
Metro: Monastiraki.

The Goulandris Museum

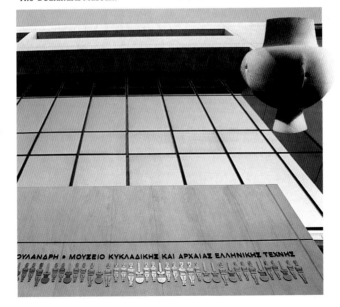

◆◆
ODION IRÓDOU ATTIKOU (ODEON OF HEROD ATTICUS)
Dhionissou Areopayitou
This fine Roman theatre, originally built by Herod Atticus of Marathon in AD161, is best seen from the Akropolis above. The restored theatre is open only during the summer festival when it makes a wonderful setting for drama and music.
Bus: 230.

◆◆◆
OLYMPION DHIOS (TEMPLE OF OLYMPIAN ZEUS)
Leoforos Olgas (tel: 922–6330)
Only 15 columns remain of what was the largest temple in Greece, yet the site retains its power. Building began in the 6th century BC, but was finished by the Emperor Hadrian only in about AD130. The temple is best seen as the sun rises behind the pillars, or floodlit at night.
Open: Tuesday to Sunday 08.30–15.00hrs.
Closed: public holidays.
Bus: 230, 024.

◆
PÍLI ADRIANOÚ (HADRIAN'S ARCH)
Leoforos Amalias
Believed to stand on the site of a 6th-century BC city gate, Hadrian's Arch marks the boundary between the ancient city, on the Akropolis side, and his own new Roman city, in which the Temple stood. Accordingly, the inscription on one side says 'This is Athens, the ancient city of Theseus', while that on the other reads,

'This is the City of Hadrian and not of Theseus.'
Bus: 024, 230.

◆◆◆
PLÁKA
The Plaka district is often denigrated as a tourist trap, but as one of the older parts of modern Athens, it is still an exciting and lively place. While you cannot avoid the main shopping streets of Kidhathineon and Adhrianou,

One of the Plaka's many tavernas

find time, too, to walk up towards the Akropolis, into the back streets where a village-like atmosphere still exists. The shopping is predominantly of the tourist variety, some shops being almost warehouse-like in capacity, but next door to a souvenir emporium you are quite likely to find a tiny drinks shop, or an unusual specialist such as a sandal-maker. Pláka is a place to visit not once but many times, at night as well as by day.

◆
PLATIA OMONIA (OMONIA SQUARE)

In Greek *omonia* means concord, but here you will find concord of a peculiarly Greek kind: heavy traffic, busy shops, a metro station, offices, coffee-houses, hotels and constant milling throngs of workers, tourists and street vendors. It can be an attraction or a headache, depending on whether you want to savour Greek city life or are simply trying to cross to the other side. In the centre are cafés and an attempt at a fountain and some greenery, but their half-hearted nature only emphasises that this is the rough side of Athens, especially at night when Omonia is the haunt of prostitutes from the nearby red-light district. Around the square are several old-fashioned coffee-houses, where the atmosphere is an equal mix of smoke and argument, and almost as noisy as outside. For a quieter

refuge, try the Bretania café at the junction of Omonia and Athinas. A *chocolatina* (chocolate gateau) or *baklava* washed down with *café au lait* or hot chocolate has excellent restorative powers for tired sightseers.

◆◆
PLATIA SINDAGMA (SYNTAGMA SQUARE)

If Athens has a heart, it is here. Much of what goes on in the square, with its hotels, cafés, kiosks, banks and offices, is geared to visitors. Airport and other buses stop near here, and with most of the main attractions a short walk away, Sindagma will probably become as familiar as the Parthenon on the skyline. At the top of the square is the Greek *Vouli* (Parliament building), in front of which the Changing of the Guards takes place hourly (but at 11.00hrs only on Sundays). This ceremony, with the soldiers known as *Evzones* in their colourful costumes, should not be missed.

◆◆
POLEMIKO MOUSÍO (WAR MUSEUM OF GREECE)

Leoforos Vasilissis Sofias 22 (tel: 729–0543/4)
It is difficult to miss this building: Spitfires and Tiger Moths are on display outside. Inside is a large collection on several spacious floors, covering every aspect of war in Greece from the ancient Trojan Wars to the Battle for Crete during World War II. It is best to start at the top and work down. Look out for some

effective 3-D models of various battle scenes. Admission is free, and there is a basement café.
Open: Tuesday to Saturday 09.00–14.00hrs, Sunday and holidays 09.30–14.00hrs.
Bus: 234.

◆◆
STADION (OLYMPIC STADIUM)
Leoforos Ardhittou
Also known as the Panathenaic Stadium, this was built in 1896 for the revival of the Olympic Games. Appropriately it was on the site, and in the form, of the ancient Panathenaic Stadium, where games had been held from the 4th century BC.
While there is little to see, the smooth white marble lines of its 47 tiers of seats (able to hold more than 60,000 spectators) are visually impressive. The running track is popular with jogging Athenians. Access is free.
Open: daily, dawn to dusk.
Bus: 2, 4, 11, 12.

◆
THÉATRO DHIONISSOU (THEATRE OF DIONYSUS)
Leoforos Dhionissou Areopayitou (tel: 322–4625)
Standing below the Akropolis on its southern slopes, this theatre, dating from the 4th century BC, was the site for an annual drama festival. Here the citizens of Athens would witness the premières of plays by Aristophanes, Sophocles and other great classical dramatists. There are amusingly detailed Dionysian statues to be seen supporting

the stage, with marble barriers from the times when wild animals fought in the arena.
Open: Monday and Wednesday to Saturday 09.00–14.45hrs, Sunday and holidays 09.00–13.45hrs.
Bus: 230.

◆
VIVLIOTHÍKI ADRIANOÚ (LIBRARY OF HADRIAN)
Eolou
This group of buildings near the Agora was constructed by the Emperor Hadrian some time after AD132 to house not only his library but also a courtyard with a central pool flanked by 100 columns. The courtyard has been closed for some time for excavation. When it is reopened it will be possible to see the library with its recesses for the rolled manuscripts of books.
Metro: Monastiraki.

◆◆
VIZANDINÓ MOUSÍO (BYZANTINE MUSEUM)
Leoforos Vasilissis Sofias 22 (tel: 723–1570)
Here another of Athens' fascinating specialist collections is delightfully housed in an 1840 villa with its own flowered courtyard. The bulk of the collection is made up of Byzantine icons, many in glorious reds and golds, while elsewhere there are bibles and mosaics, a reconstruction of an early Christian basilica and a complete recreated Byzantine church.
Open: Tuesday to Sunday 08.30–15.00hrs.
Bus: 234.

PRACTICAL ATHENS

The Theatre of Dionysus could seat 17,000 people in 64 tiers

Accommodation

One feature of Athens that makes it very practical for visitors is the wide range of excellent medium-priced hotels. There are many in or on the edge of the Plaka district, with most of the main attractions within walking distance. If, on the other hand, you require the comfort and facilities that only a top hotel can provide, then Athens has no lack of these either.

Adonis, Kodrou 3 (tel: 3249–737). Set in a quiet pedestrianised Plaka street, with a rooftop bar/breakfast room looking out at the Akropolis. Extremely helpful staff, well-furnished rooms. Inexpensive.

Astir Palace, Platia Sindagma (tel: 3643–112). Huge rooms, a marble staircase and mosaic walls make elegant surroundings for luxurious facilities. Expensive.

Athenian Inn, Haritos 22 (tel: 7238–097). In the smart Kolonaki district. Some rooms look out on Likavitos, and, like the hotel, are traditionally furnished in Greek-village style. Moderate.

Athens Hilton, Vasilissis Sofias 46 (tel: 7220–201). Airline offices and banks surround gnarled olive trees in the courtyard entrance. The marbled interior is spectacular to see. All rooms have city views, and the restaurants and swimming pool are not the least of the attractions. Expensive.

Grande Bretagne, Platia Sindagma (tel: 3230–251). This modernised but old-fashioned and distinguished hotel boasts past guests as notable as Sir Winston Churchill, Richard Strauss and Elizabeth Taylor. Expensive.

Nefeli, Yperidou 16 (tel: 3228–044). A quietly located, small family-run hotel in the Plaka, with pleasant rooms. Inexpensive.

ATHENS

Restaurants

There are mediocre as well as excellent restaurants in Athens, so it is best to stick to recommendations. Most people make for the Plaka, where there are almost as many tavernas as tourists. The best atmosphere is often in inexpensive basement restaurants such as **To Ypogeio tis Plakas**, Kidhathineon 10, or **Bakalarakia**, Kidhathineon 41 (open evenings, but closed in high summer). Establishments of this kind may not be eye-catching from the outside but they will probably be packed inside, as often as not with Greeks.

Eden, Flessa 3 (tel: 3248–858). Vegetarian restaurant in a rustic-style upstairs room. Wide menu includes meat-free moussaka and typical Greek home-cooked dishes such as bureki (courgettes and potatoes topped with feta). Closed Tuesday. Moderate.

Gerofinikas, Pindharou 10 (tel: 3636–710/3622–719). Greek Oriental-style food: chicken with pine kernels and currant pilaf could be served alongside a traditional mouskari (veal with vegetables, baked in a paper bag). Booking essential. Open lunchtimes and evenings. Expensive.

O Platanos, Dioyenous 4. The smell from the grill fills the square around the ancient plane tree that gives this famous Athens eating place its name. Outdoor tables in summer. Open lunchtimes and evenings except Sunday. Moderate.

Ta Nissia, at the Athens Hilton (tel: 7220–201). Hard to beat for more formal meals, with international and Greek dishes. Booking recommended. Closed July and August. Expensive.

Xynos, Angelou Geronda (tel: 3221–065). Tucked away since 1936 in a tiny alley and popular with Athenians. The inside may appear not to have been decorated since it opened, but that does not detract from the good simple dishes and lively nightly music. Open evenings except Sunday. Moderate.

Shopping

Athens is adequate rather than exciting as a shopping city. Most quality shops for clothing and jewellery are concentrated in the desirable Kolonaki area, between the *Vouli* (Parliament building) and Likavitos. More reasonably priced silver and gold items can be found in the old silversmiths' quarter, on Leka and Praxitelous streets. For something recognisably Greek, try the Centre of Hellenic Tradition (page 28) or museum shops, which often stock art and craft items, as well as reproductions of pieces from their own collections. Shops in the Plaka offer everything from the cheapest souvenirs to expensive antiques. Many of the larger tourist shops appear to be offering identical mass-produced goods, but it may be worth enquiring inside for exclusive work by particular artists or craftsmen. Above all, haggle. It is expected.

AROUND ATHENS

To visitors who arrive at Athens airport and immediately head into the city, it might seem that the suburbs go on forever and there could be little of interest outside the ancient heart of the capital. Yet if you were to head away from the city you would soon see a more traditional and quite different Greece: a land of coastal towns and villages separated by long stretches of impressive hilly scenery, with quiet coves and beaches. While none of the surrounding attractions fall into the 'must see' category, most are easily accessible either by public transport or on organised day trips. Many hotels and travel agents in Athens offer trips to any of the following places, but do not overlook the possibility of making your own arrangements. Bus services are usually good, regular and extremely cheap, and can also offer more flexibility on timing. Another option is to hire a taxi for a few hours, though do this only with a taxi driver recommended by your hotel,

AROUND ATHENS

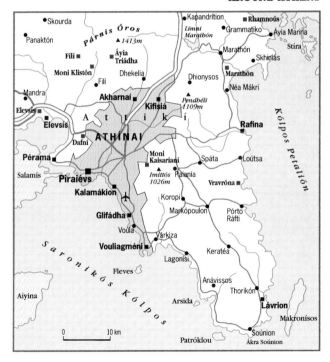

or whom you know to be reliable.

If you hire a car at the airport, you could be at Akra Sounion (Cape Sounion) after less than an hour's drive, much of it along a pleasant coastal road. You might look at the temple here, then visit Vravrona (Brauron), Marathon and Rhamnous – all easily accessible within a day. The other two sites mentioned, Dafni and Elevsis, are less than 10km apart to the west of the city, and can easily be visited on the way to or from the Peloponnese, or by bus from the centre of Athens.

Picnic lunches are recommended: Cape Sounion is the only place with adequate hotel and restaurant facilities.

ÁKRA SOÚNION (CAPE SOUNION)

65km southeast of Athens (tel: 0292–39363)

The most dramatic way to see Cape Sounion for the first time is from the Athens coastal road: turn a bend and suddenly, in the distance, the magnificent Temple of Poseidon appears, standing high on its headland. The slow approach helps build a sense of its splendid isolation and smooth lines.

The temple was built in 444BC. Today, almost 2,500 years later, Athenians still make the trip to watch the sun go down beyond its 15 remaining columns, one of which bears the scratched initials of the English poet and Graecophile Lord Byron. Visitors can no longer see these, however, as the temple is roped off to help preserve it

from the depredations of countless visitors.

Open: daily, 08.30hrs–sunset.

Bus: Buses marked 'Σουνιο' leave the terminal at 260 Odhos Liossion, Athens, hourly between 06.30 and 18.30hrs, returning 06.30–20.00hrs. The journey time is 90 minutes. There are also departures on the hour, but these buses go by the inland rather than the coastal road.

Accommodation and Restaurants

Aegaeon (tel: 0292–39262). Set on the bay, a 10-minute walk below the temple, this hotel has 45 clean, moderately priced rooms and a good restaurant. For a more inexpensive meal, try one of the tavernas overlooking the water near by. Snacks and drinks are also available at the site itself.

DAFNÍ (DAPHNI)

10km west of central Athens (tel: 01–581–1558)

The 11th-century monastery at Dafni contains some of the best-preserved church mosaics in all Greece. The holy figures glisten with gold, the dome showing Christ Pantocrator, while immediately below it are the Annunciation, the birth of Jesus, His Baptism and the Transfiguration. The mosaics are the main attraction in what is a pleasant but not outstanding site: the rest of the monastery is tiny and much of it is closed. The once-peaceful setting is now only a short distance from the multi-lane Athens-Corinth highway. The site was once a sanctuary to Apollo, for whom

Sounion: the Temple of Poseidon

the laurel, or *daphnae*, was sacred. A hint of its pagan origins returns from July to September when it is the scene for a festival of wine-tasting, accompanied by food, music and dancing.

Open: usually Tuesday to Sunday, 08.30–17.00hrs, but variable.
Closed: public holidays.
Bus: 873 from Odhos Dheliyiorgi, every 30 minutes between 06.00 and 21.00hrs.

◆
ELEVSÍS (ELOUSIS)
20km west of central Athens (tel: 01–554–6019)

It is hard to believe as you arrive at this site, with the busy coastal highway on one side and petrol refineries around, that you are standing on the original Elysian Fields. Among the most important devotional sites of Ancient Greece, this was the home of a mysterious cult, whose rites, in homage to the goddess Demeter, were so secret that scholars can only speculate about them. At its peak in the 5th century BC, the cult attracted up to 30,000 followers who would gather annually in Athens and walk down the Sacred Way, which ended here. Despite its setting, the site still has some of its ancient magic, though it is more for the dedicated historian than the casual traveller.

Foundations, pathways and fallen stones are all that remain. A small museum has the usual collection of relics and statuary from the site. Two interesting reconstructions of the sanctuary as it was help restore a little of the sense of history.

Open: Tuesday to Saturday 08.30–17.00hrs, Sunday 08.30–15.00hrs.
Closed: public holidays.
Bus: 853 or 862; regular service from Platia Eleftherias.

MARATHÓN

41km northeast of Athens
The name of Marathon has a fame far beyond its present interest to the visitor – this is a place to see if you are near by rather than one that merits a special trip. Marathon's fame in Greek history is as the site of a famous battle, in 490BC, when the Greeks defeated the Persians. Allegedly, a Greek soldier ran to the centre of Athens with news of the victory, then died on the spot. The heroic tale of a heroic victory is remembered in the modern marathon race, equal in distance to the 41km between Athens and Marathon. A mound marks the place where the 192 Athenian soldiers who died in the battle (as against a reported 6,400 Persians) were buried. A small museum, a few minutes' walk away, contains some interesting items, such as carved gravestones, a 5th-century BC boundary stone, and unusual funerary urns. Walk up the track beside the museum for a panoramic view of the fertile open plain below.
Open: museum Tuesday to Sunday, 08.30–15.00hrs.
Closed: public holidays.
Bus: hourly from Odhos Mavromation, (orange bus marked 'Μαραθωνασ').

RHAMNOÚS

50km northeast of Athens
This small, remote site is often overlooked, yet it is a delightful place amid groves of vines and olives, where the only other visitors are likely to be birds and butterflies, which abound here. In truth there is very little to see – the base of the Temple of Themis, with columns no more than a metre or two high, and the remains of the never-completed larger Temple of Nemesis. However, its isolation at the end of a rough and bumpy track gives a sense of discovering the place for yourself – a pleasing and all-too-rare feeling.
Open: Tuesday to Sunday, 08.30–15.00hrs
Closed: public holidays.
Not accessible by public transport.

VRAVRÓNA (BRAURON)

near the village of Vravrona, 25km east of Athens (tel: 0294–71020)
Pleasantly situated below a hill near the marshy coast, the ancient site of Brauron is known mainly for the Sanctuary of Artemis, thought to have been built between 2000 and 1600BC. Artemis was the goddess of fertility as well as being the patron of unmarried girls and chastity. Also here is a tiny late-Byzantine chapel and still-flowing sacred spring.
About 15 minutes' walk away is an attractive modern museum of finds from the site. Several small statues are on display in an appealing open courtyard, while inside one of the main exhibits is a reconstructed model of the Temple of Artemis.
Open: Tuesday to Sunday, 08.30–15.00hrs.
Closed: public holidays.
Bus: 304 from Athens to Artemi, then a 2km walk.

THESSALONÍKI AND THE NORTH

Greece's two northern provinces of Thraki (Thrace) and Makedhonia (Macedonia) present faces of Greece that would surprise visitors who are familiar only with the islands. Thraki shares its borders with Turkey and, much as the Greeks like to distance themselves from their eastern neighbour, the Turkish influences are clearly visible. Mosques, minarets, busy bazaars and more eastern modes of dress are all to be seen in such fascinating towns as Xanthi and Komotini, and are even more noticeable as you venture out into the rural villages.

Thraki is also a reminder that Greece's livelihood depends on more than tourism alone. At harvest time, loaded lorries by the hundred head for the markets from vast fields of cotton and tobacco. In the

Kastoria on its mountain-ringed lake

cooler mountain regions of northern Makedhonia, the delightful lakeside town of Kastoria has built its wealth on the fur trade.

This is not to say that tourism plays little part in this area. The huge province of Makedhonia also includes the Khalkidhiki peninsula, which includes some of the most developed resorts and hotel complexes in the land, yet typically enough in this country of contrasts also includes the Holy Mountain, Ayion Oros (Mount Athos). The capital of Makedhonia is Thessaloniki, Greece's second city. Its position on the waterfront makes it a more attractive proposition for visitors than many comparable cities. Its Archaeological Museum is also among the best in Greece. As with everywhere in Greece, ancient and modern coexist side by side.

◆
ALEXANDHROÚPOLIS
in the extreme northeast, on the coast

This is the last major stop on the route east to Turkey – and a very pleasant one. A wide promenade runs alongside the long stretch of beach, with children's playgrounds and other amenities. At night coloured lights illuminate the fountains and the town's dominant feature, its lighthouse, shines out. On summer evenings the locals stroll up and down in their *volta* while food stalls do a brisk trade. Across from the beach is a line of cafés, amusement arcades and souvenir shops. In the warren of narrow back streets beyond, you will find everything from jewellery to junk – an excellent place to hunt for presents. From the small harbour at Alexandhroupolis, ferries run to the little-known and mountainous island of Samothraki.

Accommodation
Egnatia (tel: 0551–28661). In its own grounds at the western end of the seafront. Clean, convenient and quiet. Moderate.

Restaurant
I Neraidha, Platia Polytekhniou. A large, smart and popular restaurant. Closed in winter. Moderate. Several others in this small square are open all year.

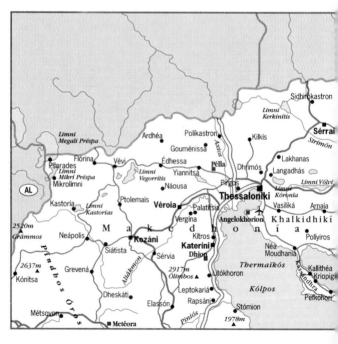

DHION
south of Katerini

The best classical site in Makedhonia, the sacred city of the Makedhonians is beautifully situated on the coastal plain beneath Mount Olympos. Visit the museum in the village, particularly for the excellent explanatory video. There are some impressive statues, well preserved by the mud that engulfed Dhion after an earthquake, and a collection of gravestones. One – that of a carpenter – depicts his axe, and another has a family of four with a capsized ship.

The site itself is a short drive from the museum. Look for the long cobbled pavement which led to Mount Olympos, the beautiful marble and mosaic floors of the well-preserved great baths, and, across the road, the Sanctuary of Isis. Here, copies of the original statues peer out through lush greenery. Kingfishers, wagtails and other birds live around the streams that flow through the site.
Open: museum and site Monday 12.30–19.00hrs, Tuesday to Friday 08.00–19.00hrs, Saturday and Sunday 08.30–15.00hrs.
Closed: public holidays.

THESSALONIKI AND THE NORTH

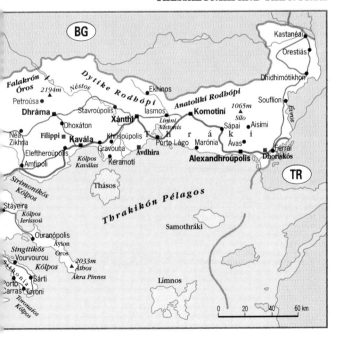

Kastoria's folklore museum

◆◆◆
KASTORÍA ✓

northwestern Greece, near the Albanian border
One of the most delightful towns in Greece, Kastoria is sited on a peaked peninsula jutting into a huge lake. The distant shores, wooded and mountainous, surround the town with natural beauty. Its only drawback is its chaotic traffic.

Kastoria is far wealthier than you might expect for a town in the remote northern mountains of Greece. It owes this to fur trade. Scraps of cheap imported fur were turned into coats here and sold overseas at a handsome profit. Many of the original mansions of the rich fur families can still be seen, in particular the **Mansion of Nerantzis Aivazis**, in Odhos Lazou. This is now an unmissable folklore museum, refurnished to show the grand mansion as it was.
Open: daily 08.30–18.00hrs.
Also worth exploring in Kastoria are the many beautifully decorated little Byzantine churches.

Accommodation
Xenia du Lac, Platia Dhexamenis (tel: 0467–22565). An 'A' class hotel, not on the lake but high in the town . Expensive.

Restaurant
Omonia, Platia Omonias. A real Greek 'come-into-the-kitchen' place, offering excellent value with hearty fish soups, bean stews and meat dishes. Cheap.

◆
FILIPPI

between Kavalla and Dhrama
A century before St Paul preached here, this historic city was the site of the Battle of Filippi. Here, in 42 BC , Mark Antony's armies beat those of Caesar's assassins, Brutus and Cassius. Visitors to Filippi today can see the remains of a theatre from the 4th century BC, two basilicas, a market-place, a temple and a large number of well-preserved marble seats from the public toilet!
Open: site Tuesday to Sunday, 08.30–15.00hrs; museum Tuesday to Sunday, 08.30–17.00hrs.
Closed: public holidays.
Bus: from Kavalla the bus to Dhrama (every 30 minutes) will stop at the site.

◆◆
KAVÁLA
on the coast east of Thessaloniki
The attractions of this bustling port may not be immediately obvious, but its appeal grows and it has plenty of interest. In addition to the fascinating markets, do not miss the **archaeological museum** (Odhos Erithrou Stavrou), whose spacious rooms on two floors include a fine jewellery display (note, especially, some delicate golden olive wreaths) and some busts from the 4th century BC whose original colouring is still intact. Kavala also has a **folk art museum** (Odhos Filippou), with paintings and sculptures by local artists as well as the usual displays of folk costumes and domestic items.

Look out for the Turkish aqueduct which runs through the town, leading into the old Turkish quarter around the **Byzantine Citadel**. Here you will find a statue to Mehmet Ali and the house in which he was born in 1769. Ring the bell and the caretaker will show you around the harem and other rooms. Mehmet Ali became Pasha of Egypt, the first in a long modern Egyptian dynasty which ended with King Farouk.
Open: archaeological museum Tuesday to Sunday 08.30–15.00hrs; folk art museum daily 09.00–11.00hrs and 18.00–21.00hrs; citadel daily, 10.00–19.00hrs.

Accommodation
Galaxy, Odhos Venizelou 15 (tel: 051–224521). A large international-style hotel, right on the harbour. Moderate.

Restaurants
O Faros, Odhos Theodhorou Poulidhou. This simple, cheap taverna specialising in fresh fish is one of several lively eating places in this street. The more sophisticated restaurants are along the harbour. Of these, the **Zafira** (expensive) is recommended by locals.

◆◆
KHALKIDHIKÍ (HALKIDIKI)
immediately southeast of Thessaloníki
Khalkidhiki is the place to go if you want either to find the crowds or (males only) to escape them totally by staying in a monastery. Seemingly one long beach resort stretches from the outskirts of Thessaloniki down the coast to the tip of **Kassandhra**, the westernmost of Khalkidhiki's three peninsular 'fingers' which poke into the Aegean Sea. The central peninsula, **Sithonia**, is slightly less busy, and more scenically attractive, but the monks of **Mount Athos** have the most dramatic landscape on their self-governed third peninsula, which is closed to the general public.

On Kassandhra there is little to choose between the various resorts. Some, such as **Kallithea**, are large while others, such as **Pefkohori** and **Kriopigi**, are smaller, but all cater to the holiday trade and are buzzing in summer: hotels, restaurants, beach bars, car hire, souvenirs, windsurfing... all the holiday trappings are here.

The central peninsula, Sithonia, can easily be driven around in a day, and if you choose to do this then make the journey in a clockwise direction for the best views of the neighbouring peninsula of Mount Athos. Sithonia has a less crowded feel than Kassandhra. Resorts do not yet encroach on each other, and there are fewer large hotels. Fine deserted stretches of beach are still to be found. A particularly good and not-too-busy beach is at **Toroni**, in the southwest corner – a full 2km of curving sand, with a few tavernas, some of which offer basic rooms to rent. If you prefer company and nightlife, the sophisticated holiday complex of **Porto Carras** is further north. By contrast, on the eastern coast facing Mount Athos, the road runs for 30km from Vourvourou to Sarti without a single town or village, just a handful of campsites and some of the best beaches in Khalkidhiki.

All most people will see of the Holy Mountain, **Mount Athos**, is a distant view from a beach or a slightly closer look by taking a boat trip round the peninsula. These offer tantalising glimpses of some of the ancient monasteries that cling to the cliffs of the 'monks' republic'. The wooded, mountainous peninsula remains totally unspoilt, with an area similar to Sithonia or Kassandhra but containing only the monasteries, which date back to the 10th and 11th centuries. Trips can be booked at most of the major Khalkidhiki resorts, and generally leave from **Ouranopolis**, the last resort before the frontier.

Visiting Mount Athos

Women are absolutely forbidden to visit Mount Athos and its 20 monasteries, while hopeful males must apply for permission. Each of the two Ministries mentioned below, in Athens and Thessaloniki, is allowed to issue only 10 permits per day, covering requests from all around the world.

The first step is to obtain a letter of recommendation from your own embassy or consulate in Athens or Thessaloniki, then take this to either the Ministry of Foreign Affairs in Athens (Zalakosta 2) or the Ministry of Makedhonia and Thraki in Thessaloniki (Platia Dhikitiriou) to exchange for a visitor's permit. This will allow you up to four days on Mount Athos, but may have a start date several weeks away.

Accommodation

Alexander Beach, near Kriopigi (tel: 0374–22433). Large, self-contained hotel with all modern comforts. Expensive.

Diaporos, Vourvourou (tel: 0375–91313). 'B' class hotel with 33 rooms. Moderate.

Kassandhra Palace, near Kriopigi (tel: 0374–51471). Plush, 'A' class hotel with lush gardens, its own taverna, and watersports facilities. Expensive.

Porto Carras, west coast of Sithonia (tel: 0375–71380). Described as the Greek Marbella, this expensive and planned resort has conference facilities, shopping arcades...

even its own vineyard and orange groves. Three separate hotels here range from the luxury **Meliton** (expensive) to the 'B' class **Village Inn** (moderate). Book well in advance for a stay in July or August.

Xenia, at the tip of the Kassandhra peninsula (tel: 0374–92277). Well-situated 'B' class hotel. Moderate.

◆◆
KOMOTINÍ
inland in northeastern Greece
This bustling Byzantine-influenced town has much beneath its modern surface to recommend it. Its bazaar area, to the north and east of the main square, Platia Ireni, is a fascinating labyrinth of streets and shops. The fish, meat and fruit markets are busy any day but packed on Tuesdays when people from surrounding villages flock to the town.
The **Museum of Folk Life and History** on Odhos Ayios Yiorgos is especially worth a visit. The collection of domestic items and folk costumes includes fine examples of the local embroidery known as Tsevres, traditionally offered by the bride's family in Thracian wedding rites.
Open: Monday to Saturday, 10.00–13.00hrs.
The **archaeological museum** is set back from the main road to Xanthi. Its wide-ranging collection includes copies of cave drawings, painted sarcophagi, and information about the nearby ancient sites of Avdhira and Maronia.
Open: daily, 09.00–17.00hrs.

Accommodation
Democritus, Platia Viziniou 8 (tel: 0531–22579). Probably the best value of several hotels aimed at Komotini's many business visitors.

An antique shop in Komotini

◆
MARÓNIA
south of Komotini

From the tucked-away farming village of Maronia, take the turning marked Ayios Haralambos and bump along a rutted track to see the appealing ruins of what was, during the Classical period, a substantial city. The remains of a temple are hidden among olive groves, while nearby is a village-scale theatre. Most of its seating is still intact, along with parts of the stage and support columns. A wall around the arena protected spectators in the days of Roman contests involving wild animals. Today the theatre is still occasionally used for more conventional shows, in this magnificent peaceful setting looking out over groves of trees to the sea. *Open*: at all times.

◆◆
NÉSTOS VALLEY
northeast of Thessaloniki

The Nestos valley is best approached from Dhrama, by heading out on the Kavala road and taking the left fork for Stavroupolis. The most dramatic views are beyond Stavroupolis, on the approach to Xanthi. Leaving Dhrama, the road climbs gently with the peaks of the Rodhopi range, across the boarder in Bulgaria, to the left. The road passes through villages which look like the most remote in Greece, hidden away – and indeed sometimes cut off – in this high mountain pass. The road crosses the Nestos river, with views of sweeping forests and mountain slopes on either side, and climbs to a more thickly wooded and more thinly populated area, past the occasional small village. The final stretch is through the gorge that heads south and down into Xanthi and back to civilisation. This is truly a memorable drive, but the road is sometimes closed by snow in winter.

◆◆◆
ÓROS ÓLIMBOS (MOUNT OLYMPOS)
north of Larisa

Unless you are a keen and fit walker or climber you must be content with looking at Mount Olympos, though it makes a magnificent sight. The cluster of peaks, usually shrouded in cloud, rears up from a narrow plain between mountains and sea. The wooded slopes of Olympos are clearly visible from the main Athens–Thessaloniki road. To the south the road heads inland into the lush Vale of Tempe, the pass where the Pinios river separates Olympos from its neighbour, Mount Ossa. The name Olimbos (Olympos) applies to the entire range, whose highest peak – the highest in Greece – is Mitikas (2,917m), also usually referred to as Olimbos (Olympos). This was the legendary home of the Greek gods and indeed was not scaled by man until 1913. Today, in summer at least, it is a tough but manageable two-day challenge for experienced, fit and well-equipped hill walkers. The Hellenic Climbing Club in nearby Litokhoron can arrange for you to hire a guide or stay in a mountain refuge.

Olympos's canyon of Marrolongos

Accommodation
Mirto, Christofoulos Foundas, Litokhoron (down from the main square; tel: 0352–81398). A good 'A' class hotel with modern, well-equipped rooms. Moderate.

Restaurant
Dhamaskinia, Odhos Vasilios Konstantinos. Up the hill from the fast-food places on Litokhoron's main square, here is a real Greek taverna offering a good selection of fish, meat and salad dishes. Inexpensive.

◆◆
PÉLLA
northwest of Thessaloniki
Typically Greek, this historic site is on one side of a busy main road, with the museum on the other and little parking space. However, the ancient royal city of Pella is well worth visiting for its mosaics, which are among the finest in Greece. Some can still be seen *in situ* and others in the museum. The colours are fading on some, but they are still full of life and vitality, depicting a lion hunt and other scenes which once decorated floors and walls in what was the capital of Makedhonia, home of Philip II of Makedhonia, and birthplace of Alexander the Great.
Open: site and museum Tuesday to Sunday 08.30–15.00hrs.
Closed: public holidays.

◆◆◆
PRÉSPA, LÍMNI (PRESPA LAKES)
northwest of Kastoria
A visit to the Prespa Lakes, hidden away in a magnificently remote and stunningly beautiful part of northwest Greece, is a treat to be savoured. In the distance to the north are the snow-capped peaks of wha was Yugoslavia, to the we mountains of Albania. P

is a quiet fishing village on the shores of the larger of the two lakes (Megali Prespa) – a delightful stop, perhaps for a meal of fresh fish at one of its tiny tavernas. Another fishing village, **Mikrolimni**, stands on the shore of the smaller lake (Mikri Prespa), whose southern tip is in Albania. This lake's protected reed-beds are home to many species of birds such as egrets, pelicans, ducks and grebes (see also page 94). The whole area is lacking in tourist facilities – this, indeed, is part of its appeal. There is a post office and a taverna in the only other village, **Ayios Yermanos**. Some basic but cheap rooms are available to rent in each of the three villages.

◆◆
THESSALONÍKI (THESSALONIKA or SALONIKA)

If you arrive in Greece's second city after visiting quieter regions, its noise and size will hit you like a brick. However, it has many attractions and its waterfront setting goes a long way to compensate for the traffic and pollution. Thessaloniki also has a wealth of museums and historical buildings, cosmopolitan shopping and nightlife, and enough interesting restaurants to satisfy the most jaded diner. Any visit must take in the **Arkheologiko Mousio** (**archaeological museum**) on Platia Hanti (tel: 031–830–538). Thessaloniki being the capital of

THESSALONIKI

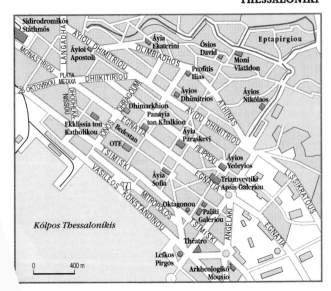

Ayia Sofia, a former mosque

Makedhonia, its museum houses finds from Makedhonian tombs, with a special display of treasures unearthed at Vergina (see page 54). Here can be seen gold masks to rival those from Mycenae, golden crowns and wreaths, and gold statuettes – an exciting collection.
Open: Monday 10.30–19.00hrs, Tuesday to Friday 08.00–19.00hrs, Saturday and Sunday 08.30–15.00hrs.
Closed: public holidays.
Another excellent example of its kind is the **Laografico - Ethnologiko Mousio Makedhonias** (**Ethnological Museum of Makedhonia**) at Odhos Vassilias Olgas 68 (tel: 031–830–591). This has a comprehensive collection of elaborate folk costumes, day-to-day household items, spinning and weaving displays, weapons, and accounts of rural and religious festivals – all explained in English and Greek.
Open: Friday to Wednesday, 09.30–14.00hrs.
Closed: public holidays.

A third museum is housed in one of the city's major landmarks, the tower called **Lefkos Pirgos** (the White Tower), on the waterfront. The tower was built in the 16th century, and is known as the site where Turkish soldiers massacred Christians in 1826, earning it the alternative name of 'Bloody Tower'. Inside is a small but interesting collection of coins, icons, jewellery and mosaics, on five floors, leading up to the roof, 32m high, which offers a good view of the city.
Open: Monday 12.30–19.00hrs, Tuesday to Friday 08.30–19.00hrs, Saturday and Sunday 08.30–15.00hrs.
Closed: public holidays.
A further Thessaloniki landmark is the **Rotonda**, also known as the church of Ayios Yeoryios. Built in Roman times as an imperial mausoleum, it later became a Christian church, then a mosque, and is now only occasionally in use for exhibitions.
Thessaloniki has many other fascinating churches, including the largest church in Greece, **Ayios Dhimitrios**. This originally dated back to the 5th century, but most of it has since been destroyed and rebuilt.
The church of **Osios David** on Odhos Timotheou is a genuine 5th-century church. It has a particularly prized mosaic showing the Vision of Ezekiel. The 8th-century church and one-time mosque, **Ayia Sofia**, is another not to be missed.
For shopping, visit the **Bedestan**, the old Ottoman bazaar area off Venizelou Street.

Accommodation

There is no shortage of good hotels in all price ranges.

Esperia, Odhos Olympou 58 (tel: 031–269–321). The en-suite rooms are very comfortable, and the staff welcoming. Moderate.

Park, Odhos Dhragoumi 81 (tel: 031–524–121). Also modern and well-equipped, but small and friendly. Moderate.

Restaurants

Limaniotis, Navarhou Votsi 1–3. A seafood-only restaurant near the harbour, with regular live music and a great atmosphere. Closed Sunday. Expensive.

Olymbos Naoussa, Nikis 5 (tel: 031–275–715). Only open at lunchtimes, when it is usually packed with locals enjoying its elegant surroundings, sea views and specialities such as *midia tiganita* (fried mussels). Moderate.

◆

VERGÍNA

west of Thessaloniki, near Veroia

Near the remote village of Vergina, several Makedhonian sites are among the most significant Greek finds of this century. They are the tombs of King Philip II and other members of the Makedhonian royal family. Finds from the tombs are housed in the Archaeological Museum in Thessaloniki (see page 52–3). The king's tomb is currently closed to the public as it is still being excavated. Further up the road, a smaller tomb is inelegantly covered by a tin shelter. The most attractive site is beyond this, at the edge of the hills. Here is the palace of

Palatitsia, whose splendidly situated ruins give a real sense of excitement at the treasures still to be discovered here. *Open*: Tuesday to Sunday, 08.30–15.00hrs. *Closed*: public holidays.

XÁNTHI

between Kavala and Komotini

This busy Thracian town has a real touch of the Orient about it, especially on Saturday when its large open-air market attracts Greeks, Turks, gypsies and Pomaks – a people whose ethnic roots are in Bulgaria, which is only about 30km north of Xanthi. This is tobacco-growing country, and many of the mansions in Xanthi's old quarter belonged to wealthy tobacco merchants. It is worth wandering around the streets of the old quarter for their old-fashioned village-like atmosphere. See, too, the bazaar area. The eastern influence shows in the grouping of similar shops: here a row of shoe shops, next a street of hardware merchants. This is close to the pleasant main square, itself lined with busy cafés and a good place to stop and stare.

Accommodation

Nestos, Leoforo Kavala (tel: 0541–27531). 'B' class hotel acceptable for an overnight visit. Moderate.

Restaurant

Kalmataria, overlooking the main square. Smart new restaurant with a wide menu. Popular both lunchtimes and evenings. Inexpensive.

CENTRAL GREECE

Central Greece is a convenient grouping together of several administrative regions, including Ipiros (Epirus) in the west, the central plains of Thessalia (Thessaly), and tongue-twisting areas such as Sterea Ellas and Aitolia kai Akarnania.

The plain of Thessalia, from which the monasteries of Meteora jut up like astonishing rock sculptures, was once an inland sea. It is therefore now very fertile and very flat. Around it, however, are some of Greece's most beautiful and dramatic mountain ranges. In the extreme south the Parnassos mountains cluster round the sacred site of Delfi. To the west the Pindhos mountains contain several of Greece's highest peaks, sweeping north to the once-remote Albanian border. Central Greece contains some of the mainland's most compelling sights, both man-made and natural. In addition to Delfi and Meteora, there is the densely wooded Pilion peninsula and the breathtaking beauty of the Vikos Gorge. A stay in the Zagorian mountain villages surrounding the gorge may make you feel you have found the true heart of Greece.

ARÁKHOVA
south of Lamia

It is hard to believe that a village could survive the twin drawbacks of having a main road straight through the centre *and* being only 11km from Delfi, yet Arakhova does retain its rugged mountain-village independence. As a base for visiting Delfi and the Parnassos mountains around, it cannot be bettered. Inevitably there are souvenir shops lining the main road, but there are also traditional houses in steep narrow lanes. In the cafés each evening, moustached men gather to talk, drink coffee and click their worry-beads.

Accommodation

Apollon, Odhos Delphon 20 (tel: 0267–31427). An excellent, small 'A' class hotel – rooms as good as you will find anywhere. Inexpensive. There is also a 'D' class Apollon, run by the same family, with more basic accommodation.

Restaurant

Taverna Karnathanassi, Odhos Delphon 56. Local wine and simple but well-cooked dishes served in typical friendly Greek fashion. Cheap.

ÁRTA
south of Ioannina

Missed by many guidebooks, Arta would well repay a stay of several days. The small and attractive capital of the region of Aitolia kai Akarnania, it is quite a young, sophisticated place for rural Greece: its cafés range from the chic Café Elegant to the archetypal Greek café not-so-elegant, where the men smoke and play rowdy games of cards. But Arta also boasts several small Byzantine churches, monasteries, busy vegetable and fish markets, and a fine setting in a loop on the Arakhthos River.

Accommodation

Amvrakia, Odhos Priovolou 13 (tel: 0642–22845). Clean and central. Inexpensive.

Xenia, Frourio (tel: 0642–28311). Situated within the grounds of the castle, hence the simple address. Undoubtedly the best hotel in Arta. Expensive.

Restaurant

Pizza Venezia, Ayios Konstantinos (tel: 0642–21678). If you feel you cannot face one more Greek salad, then eat at this smart, modern Italian restaurant, which serves a range of pasta and pizza dishes, and – a rare treat in Greece – warm bread rolls. Moderate.

♦♦♦ DELFÍ (DELPHI) ✓

south of Lamia

This has to be the single most attractive classical site in Greece, eclipsing even the Akropolis of Athens. To the Ancient Greeks, Delfi was the centre of the world. It is easy to share their feelings as you stand among its ruins and gaze at the vast valley of olive trees which rolls away like a carpet beneath your feet down to the distant sea.

Delfi is renowned for its oracle, and as you stand before the Rock of the Sibyl – the most famous oracle of them all – imagine the rows of Greek citizens come to seek guidance and help. Today, of course, it will be rows of visitors, and coaches lined up in dozens along the road, so try to stay locally and visit early or late in

the day, if possible. The site deserves some quiet attention. A detailed map and guide from the ticket office is useful.

You will see from the map that the ruins of Delfi are spread out: do not miss the **Castalian Spring** at the sharp bend in the road, and the **Gymnasium**,

CENTRAL GREECE

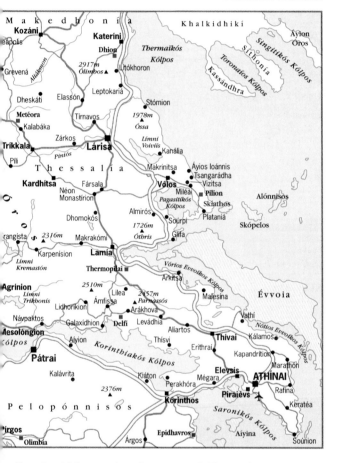

Temple of Athena and much-photographed **Tholos**, slightly further downhill.

The main site entrance leads to the **Sacred Precinct** itself, the sanctuary of Apollo, on whose behalf the priestesses would deliver their pronouncements on the seventh day of the month. The oracles were consulted by a steady stream of pilgrims for a long period – from about the 12th century BC until the 4th century AD. Delfi's most famous building is the **Temple of Apollo**, above which rises a 5,000-seat **theatre**. Up beyond this, where

fewer visitors venture, is a well-preserved 7,000-seat **stadium**. The **museum**, near the Sacred Precinct, is one of the best in Greece. It has a fine display of items from the site, including pottery, bronzes, friezes and – the highlight of the collection – the Bronze Charioteer.
Open: site Monday to Friday 07.30–17.15hrs, Saturday and Sunday 08.30–14.45hrs; museum Monday 11.00–17.15hrs, other days as above.
Closed: public holidays.
Bus: five daily from Athens. The site is within walking distance of Delfi village.

Accommodation
Olympic, Fridherikis 5 (tel: 0265–82641). The best view in Delfi. Moderate.

Restaurant
Taverna Vakhos, Apollonos 31. One of the best and one of the cheapest tavernas, with splendid views over the olive groves.

DHODHÓNI
southwest of Ioannina
Even older than Delfi, this site, dedicated to Zeus, is thought to have been used for religious purposes as long ago as 2000BC. The oracle here was consulted by kings and common citizens alike. Some of their questions are preserved on tablets now on display in the archaeological museum in Ioannina, 22km away.
Dhodhoni's theatre, one of the largest on the mainland, was beautifully reconstructed in the late 19th century and is now used for occasional summer performances. A lone tree looks down from the rim, weeds rise from the seating like spectators, and kestrels nest in the massive stone buttresses.
Open: Monday to Friday 08.00–17.00hrs, Saturday and Sunday 08.30–15.00hrs.
Closed: public holidays.
Bus: two daily from Ioannina.

The Sacred Way at Delfi

EFIRA (EPHYRA)

southwest of Ioannina, near Mesopotamo

The Necromanteion of Efira is a small and remote site, but an unusual and interesting one. It is not easily accessible by public transport, being a 5km walk from the village of Kastri.
The haunting ruins are on a small mound above what was regarded as the mouth of the River Styx, which flowed into the underworld. Accordingly, the oracle here was the Oracle of the Dead. The mound was once an island, where visitors would spend the night before seeing the oracle. Today's visitors can take the same short route through a small maze of corridors to the sanctuary. Here pilgrims were lowered into an underground chamber to come face to face with the oracle, a priestess who had to be at least 50 years old. Today the eerie descent is by metal steps.
Open: daily 08.00–15.00hrs. *Closed*: public holidays.
A day's drive could also take in two other enjoyable ancient sites to the south: **Kassopi**, magnificently situated high above the Ionian Sea, and the overgrown ruins of the important Roman city of **Nikopolis**. Both are to the north of Preveza.

IOÁNNINA

Though it is a noisy, modern town, Ioannina will repay a stay of a few days. It is beautifully situated on Lake Pamvotis, where many of its attractions are found. Not the least is the tiny island of **Nissi**, a peaceful haven in the middle of the lake. Boats leave every half-hour (hourly in winter) between 06.30 and 23.00hrs, from the harbour below the castle walls. Nissi seems not merely 10 minutes but 10 centuries away from Ioannina. In among its reed-beds are fishing boats and all over the island nightingales sing, while fishermen mend their nets. At the **Monastery of Pandhelimonos** the rebellious despot Ali Pasha was assassinated in 1822. The bullet-holes can still be seen in what is now a museum.
In Ioannina a mosque in the **Frourio**, Ali Pasha's citadel, houses a **popular art museum**, while the **archaeological museum** has a small collection including local paintings and sculptures, and items from Dhodhoni (see page 58). Ioannina's back streets hide an old bazaar area where silversmiths still work, producing the silver and turquoise jewellery for which Ioannina has long been known.
Open: art museum daily 08.00–15.00hrs; archaeological museum Tuesday to Saturday 08.30–15.00hrs; Monastery of Pandhelimonos Tuesday to Sunday 08.30–15.00hrs.

Nearby
Pérama Spiliá (the Perama Caves) extend for 2km under the hills at Perama village, 5km from Ioannina. Greece's largest cave system was discovered in 1941 by villagers seeking refuge from bombing. Guided tours point out curiously shaped stalactites and

stalagmites, such as the Sphinx and the Statue of Liberty.
Open: daily 08.00–20.00hrs summer, (16.00hrs winter).
Bus: regular service to Perama from Ioannina.

Accommodation
Olympic, Odhos Melanidou 2 (tel: 0651–25888). A comfortable, central and modern hotel. Moderate.
Pension Varvara, on Nissi (tel: 0651–24396). Basic but peaceful. Cheap.

Restaurants
Kipos Taverna, Karaiskaki 20. Outdoor tables and occasional music. Open evenings only. Moderate.
Litharitsia, Ayias Marinas. Combined rooftop café and downstairs restaurant with a bustling atmosphere. Moderate.
Taverna Propodhes, Nissi. The best of Nissi's three tavernas, though more for its setting as the seafood options are similar in all. Inexpensive.

◆
MESOLÓNGION (MISSOLONGHI)
south of Agrinion
A name long associated in literary minds with the British poet, Lord Byron, Missolonghi is a place to pass through rather than linger in. Byron died here in 1824. Today there is little to see: the poet's house was destroyed during World War II, though his statue stands among other monuments in the Garden of the Heroes, on the northwest side of the town. The huge lagoon on which Mesolongion stands is good for coastal birdwatching (see page 94).

◆◆◆
METÉORA ✓

northwest of Trikkala
You will never forget your first distant view of the rocks of Meteora thrusting up from the Thessalia plain. Like surreal dark sculptures they reach to the skies. Slowly, the tiny specks of buildings clinging to them reveal themselves to be, unbelievably, the Meteora monasteries.
Meteora means 'rocks in the air'. In fact, the rocks were once covered by the prehistoric sea that covered this plain. Their astonishing appearance is due to a combination of wave action and subsequent batterings by wind and rain. Nature's sculpting has ensured that Meteora is seldom disappointing: startling in sunlight, breathtaking in mist or twilight. Birds of prey – Egyptian

A Posthumous Hero
Lord Byron's untimely death at Missolonghi, from a fever, happened before he could contribute very much to the Greek cause in the War of Independence, other than money and good intentions. However, his widely publicised death undoubtedly focused European attention on the Greek cause and prompted many foreigners to volunteer to help it to succeed. Since that time, Byron has been something of a Greek national hero and his name (translated 'Vironos') has been given to streets and squares up and down the country.

The incredible Meteora monasteries

vultures, kestrels and buzzards – soar above this strange landscape, while closer at hand you may see blue rock-thrushes or hear them singing.

The monasteries date from the early 14th century, by which time the rocks had long been the home of hermits. It would be hard to imagine a more perfect refuge for them. One community, at **Dhoupiani**, developed as a result of visits by monks from Mount Athos, then others followed until there were 13 monasteries. They flourished until the 18th century, then began a steady decline. Today there are only a handful of monks and nuns, most of them seeing to the needs of the many visitors. Only six of the monasteries are accessible to visitors, and to visit them all you will need your own transport. If time is limited, **Mega Meteoron** (also known as the **Metamorphosis**) is the grandest,

highest, most distant and oldest of the Meteora monasteries. Its domed church is magnificent, and it also has a museum in its 16th-century one-time dining room. Nearby is the monastery of **Varlaam**, with lovely gardens and a frescoed chapel. This is also the best place to see one of the original ascent towers, in which supplies and visitors were once hauled up on a rope. The convent of **Ayia Triadha** is also worth seeing. Its spectacular setting was used as a location in the James Bond film *For Your Eyes Only*.

Visitors must dress appropriately: long trousers for men, skirts of a decent length for women, and no bare shoulders. You will not be admitted if you do not comply. All the monasteries make a small admission charge, and it is a good idea to take your own refreshments.

Open: hours vary from
monastery to monastery, so
check locally. Telephone Mega
Meteoron (0432–22278) for
details.

Accommodation
Antoniadhi, Odhos Trikalon
148, Kalabaka (tel: 0432–24387).
Centrally situated in the village
that is the main base for
exploring Meteora, this hotel
lacks views of the monasteries
but offers welcome convenience
and comfort in a place where
overcharging and poor facilities
are all too common. Moderate.

Restaurant
To Kalami, Kastraki. Dine
beneath the shadows of Meteora
at this unpretentious taverna on
the unnamed main square in
Kastraki, a village just north of
Kalabaka. Cheap.

METEORA

◆◆
MÉTSOVON
northeast of Ioannina
One of the few places in Greece
where you may see men and
women wearing traditional
costumes, Metsovon is a
delightful town more than
1,000m high on the edge of a
valley in the Pindhos mountains.
In winter a popular ski resort, in
summer a place for walkers
and climbers, its facilities are
generally good.
On sale everywhere are the
shepherds' crooks that the
elderly men carry, as well as
many other local craft items.
Blankets and rugs are a good
buy, particularly at the **Idhrima
Tositsa** (Tositsa Foundation) in
the main square. The Tositsa
family name is everywhere:
Baron Tositsas, a wealthy native
of the town who died in 1950,
left money to fund small local
industries, such as farming and
weaving, and the town's
museum. This is the **Arhondiko
Tositsa** in the main street
(Odhos Tositsa!), the restored
18th-century family mansion.
Open: Friday to Wednesday,
08.30–13.00hrs and
16.00–18.00hrs.

Accommodation
Egnatia, Odhos Tositsa 10 (tel:
0656–41263). Comfortable,
clean and (although on the main
street) quiet. The owners are
friendly and accommodating.
Moderate.

Restaurant
To Spitiko, Odhos Tositsa. Try
local dishes such as meatballs
with leeks, the local wine (*katoi*)
or one of many local cheeses,
such as *vlachotiri*. Moderate.

CENTRAL GREECE

Typical Pilion countryside

◆◆
PÁRGA

on the coast southwest of Ioannina

Parga is a most attractive beach resort, with a long stretch of almost-white sand in the town centre and two more beaches near by. The small town is therefore extremely popular. Its streets are lined with souvenir shops, but also with hibiscus and bougainvillea flowers. A ruined Venetian castle towers at one end of the main beach, and offshore is a pretty island, with trees and a little chapel. Along the front a row of tavernas beckons – a pleasant place to sit and eat, day or night.

Accommodation

Paradissos, Odhos Livadha 33 (tel: 0684–31229). Right in the centre of Parga, this hotel's facilities belie its 'D' class rating. Inexpensive.

Restaurant

To Stelio, Odhos Anesartisias. The best (by a whisker) of several tavernas offering fresh fish dishes. Moderate.

◆◆◆
PILÍON (PELION) PENINSULA ✓

roughly half-way between Athens and Thessaloniki

Visitors are slow to discover, as the Greeks already have, that this is one of the loveliest regions of Greece. Rugged and mountainous, the peninsula juts out into the Aegean towards the Sporades islands. The whole peninsula is wooded, with oak and beech forests, peach, pear and olive trees, and many different herbs and other bushes.

One approach to the Pilion is by ferry from the island of Skiathos. Otherwise the only road in is through the unattractive port of Volos, from where the Pilion is signposted. Northeast of Volos the road zig-zags skywards to the beautiful old mountain village of **Makrinitsa**. Cars must be left at the entrance to the village, whose steep, narrow cobbled streets were designed for people and donkeys only. It is picturesque but very popular, so you are unlikely to have the place to yourself.

Makrinitsa is preserved by the Greek government as a traditional village. Another such settlement is **Vizitsa**, centred on a large main square surrounded by plane trees, churches, cafés and tavernas. This, too, is a popular spot with day-trippers but the delightful peace of a mountain village in the morning and evening can be found by staying in one of the government-run guesthouses. The central reception is marked 'Reception Guesthouse' on the right as you enter (tel: 0423–86373), and this also houses a small folk museum with an idiosyncratic little collection. Snowshoes are a reminder of the chillier side of life in a mountain village.

The traditional Pilion mountain village of Makrinitsa

Other villages in the Pilion interior worth seeing include **Mileai** and **Tsangaradha**, the latter said to have the largest plane tree in Greece in its main square. You do not need to measure it to see that there could be some truth in the claim. The tree is 18m round and allegedly 1,000 years old. The Pilion is not all mountain villages: there are some very attractive beach resorts too. One of the most popular is **Ayios Ioannis**, on the east coast, at the end of a 7km switchback drive down to the sea. Its long sandy beach is ideal, and this relaxed resort has a string of waterfront tavernas and small hotels.

Accommodation
Aloe Hotel, Ayios Ioannis (tel: 0426–31421) overlooks the sea, and its design makes full use of the fact with a lovely terrace and dining room. Bedrooms are comfortable and very well

furnished. Moderate.
Arhontiko Karamarli,
Makrinitsa (tel:
0421–99570/27119). One of the
best of Makrinitsa's restored
guesthouses, expensive but
well furnished in traditional
manner, with dark wood
dressers and rugs galore.
Vergos Mansion, Vizitsa (tel:
0423–86293/86480/22207). One
of several modernised
mansions, with balconied
rooms. Expensive.

Restaurants
Ostria Taverna, Ayios Ioannis.
One of the best restaurants in
the Pilion, tucked away in a
back street but well signposted
from the beach. This smart
restaurant includes on its menu
Pilion dishes such as *kouneli
kokkinisto* (rabbit stew).
Expensive.
Pantheon, main square,
Makrinitsa. This must have one
of the best restaurant views in
Greece. Try the Pilion speciality
spedzofai, a pepper and spicy
sausage stew. Moderate.

◆
THERMOPÍLAI (THERMOPYLAE)
southeast of Lamia
It is hard to summon up a
picture of Thermopilai's
important place in history while
traffic thunders by on the
Athens-Thessaloniki motorway,
but it was here, in the Pass of
Thermopilai, that a small
Spartan army of a few hundred
soldiers fought to the death to
try to hold off 100 times as
many invading Persians in
480BC. The strategic
importance of the pass is less
evident today, as the sea which

once marked one boundary has
now receded. A heroic statue to
the King of the Spartans,
Leonidas, stands beside the
motorway, while the burial
mound of the brave Spartan
army is nearby at Loutra
Thermopilion.

◆
THÍVAI (THEBES)
northwest of Athens
Like Thermopilai, Thivai is
known more for its past (as
Ancient Thebes) than for its
present, and today is worth a
stop rather than a stay. Once
known as the Seven-Gated City,
and for a time the capital of
Greece, Thebes was also the
home of Oedipus, who had
such unfortunate parental
relationships. It was also here,
in the acropolis known as the
Kadmeia, that the Greek
alphabet was said to have been
invented.
The modern town has been
rebuilt twice after disastrous
earthquakes in 1853 and 1893.
Its few ancient remains are
scattered, mostly hidden
among the modern buildings.
Others are to be found in the
town's best feature for visitors,
the **archaeological museum** on
Odhos Pindharou. This
attractive building has a
flourishing garden and a
courtyard containing
tombstones and other
architectural fragments. Inside
is a healthy collection of
pottery, jewellery, ivory,
clothing and bronzes.
Open: Tuesday to Saturday
08.30–15.00hrs, Sunday
09.30–14.30hrs.
Closed: public holidays.

◆◆◆
ZAGORIAN VILLAGES AND THE VIKOS GORGE ✓

north of Ioannina

The area known as Zagoria, in the Pindhos mountains close to the Albanian border, is one of the loveliest regions in Europe. It owes its unspoilt nature to its rugged mountainous terrain and relative inaccessibility. Indeed, until recently, areas near the border were a closed military zone, and, in what was declared a National Park in 1975, there are still wolves and bears to be found – though the average visitor is unlikely to come across them.

Zagoria's nearest airport is at Ioannina, and that only a national one. For an international airport you must look to Preveza, on the coast about 120km south, mainly handling holiday flights to the nearby Ionian islands. Public transport is limited, although daily buses from Ioannina serve the larger Zagorian villages. But for anyone with a car Zagoria is easily reached – and certain not to disappoint. The peaks of the Pindhos, snow-capped from October to May, include Gamila (2,497m) and Smolikas, at 2,637m the second highest mountain in Greece after Olympos. The melting snows feed the lower slopes and turn them into carpets of alpine flowers in late spring and early summer, while in the skies above golden eagles and Egyptian vultures soar.

There are 46 Zagorian villages, some now inhabited by only a handful of families. Many are linked by footpaths, which typically cross mountain rivers on elegant yet sturdy stone packhorse bridges.

The villages, too, have a distinctive look. Cobbled lanes are lined with typical stone houses, some of them once grand mansions, financed by the Zagorian men who went abroad to seek work and avoid the poverty of their remote homeland. The region is still not rich, the land poor and hard to cultivate. A welcome boost will be given by the Greek government's policy of turning some of the old mansions into guesthouses for visitors. Sympathetically restored and expensively priced, one of the first such splendid buildings is the EOT guesthouse in the village of **Megalo Papingo** (tel: 0653–41615).

There are no large hotels in Zagoria – one of its attractions – but most of the larger villages will have a small family hotel or two, or accommodation of some kind, and a choice of one or two tavernas where the food will be simple but wholesome. Two such villages are Tsepelevo and Monodhendhri.

Monodhendhri is normally the setting-off point for walkers keen enough to tramp the length of the **Vikos Gorge**, a full day's hike of about 13km to Megalo Papingo. A shorter walk of about four or five hours is possible by entering the gorge at the village of Vikos, crossing it and walking to Megalo Papingo. Anyone who is reasonably fit should be able to do the full walk, though good boots, a map and food and drink are recommended. Care must be taken, and local conditions checked before starting out. When the snows melt in late spring, parts of the gorge can become inaccessible, and at any time sudden storms can bring danger, as in any mountain region. There are also a few poisonous snakes around, so take care – though they are far less likely to bite you than to flee as you approach.

Having said all that, the effort and care will be more than repaid as you walk by the river and reach those parts of the gorge where the walls tower to 1000m above you. A delightful spot is the **Voidhomatis Springs**, a convenient place for a picnic, a rest and perhaps even a brisk swim in the placid water. Your only company is likely to be the occasional tortoise or bird, with perhaps another walker or two from time to time. The Vikos Gorge is much more satisfying than the more famous Samaria Gorge in Crete: more remote, more mountainous, more Greek.

Clouds brood over the Vikos Gorge

PELOPÓNNISOS (THE PELOPONNESE)

The Peloponnese could be described as Greece's largest island, since the building of the Corinth Canal severed it from the rest of the mainland in the 1890s. Although it is possible to drive across the Peloponnese in a day, you should allow at least a week, preferably two, even to skim the surface of its contrasting attractions. The area includes Olimbia (Olympia), home of the Olympic Games, as well as other unmissable classical sites such as Mikinai (Mycenae), Epidhavros, Anaktora Nestoros (Nestor's Palace) and Ancient Korinthos (Corinth). Beach resorts, mountain villages and the walled Byzantine cities of Mistras and Monemvasia are all here to be discovered and, apart from one or two larger ports like Patrai (Patras), there is scarcely a corner in more than 20,000 sq km that fails to impress with its beauty.

The excavated palace of King Nestor

◆◆◆
ANÁKTORA NESTOROS (NESTOR'S PALACE)
southwestern Peloponnese, north of Pilos
Before visiting Nestor's Palace, see the **archaeological museum**, above the nearby village of Khora, where most of the finds from the palace are displayed. Three large rooms contain impressive collections from the various chamber tombs found on the site, displays of bone and tusk, pots from the pantry, items from the throne room, gold cups and

frescoes. There are functional items such as chimney pipes, and decorative gold jewellery that someone at King Nestor's court wore 3,000 years ago. *Open*: Tuesday to Sunday 08.30–15.00hrs.
These displays help flesh out the rather bare remains of the palace itself, discovered in 1939. The setting is beautiful, overlooking a valley of olive trees, though the site is protected by a rather unattractive large roof. A little imagination easily re-creates the legendary home of King Nestor, where, in *The Odyssey*, Telemachus, son of Odysseus, came seeking news of his father. Before feasting, Telemachus was bathed and anointed by Nestor's daughter, Polycaste; a superbly preserved bathtub was indeed found at the site.

Nearby

The best base for visiting Nestor's Palace is the pretty harbour town of **Pilos**, to the south on the vast Navarino Bay, scene of the Battle of Navarino (see page 17). The fortress of **Neo Kastro** was once used to house prisoners from feuding Maniote families (see page 77), who continued their vendettas in the prison until many separate cells were built to keep them apart. *Open*: Tuesday to Sunday 08.30–15.00hrs.

Accommodation

Karalis, Kalamatas 26, Pilos (tel: 0723–23021). Surprisingly only

The Story of Pelops

Peloponnisos – the Greek name for the Peloponnese – means 'Island of Pelops'. In Greek mythology Tantalus, father of Pelops, had invited Zeus and the other gods to a feast (possibly at Corinth), only to discover that there was not enough food in the kitchen. He therefore cut his son into pieces and added him to the stew. Zeus later revived Pelops in such splendid fashion that Poseidon immediately fell in love with the youth and carried him off to Mount Olympos.

THE PELOPONNESE

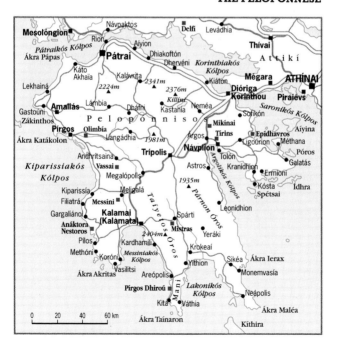

'C' class, this hotel has 'A' class facilities. The balconied front rooms have extensive views over Navarino Bay. Moderate.
Karalis Beach (tel: 0723–23031). 'B' class, with similar facilities to the Karalis, but closed in winter.

Restaurants

Philip Restaurant, on the Kalamai road in Pilos. Greek atmosphere and a good choice of grills. Moderate.
Restaurant 1930, Platia Papafleza, Pilos. Intimate bistro-style restaurant with a small, ever-changing menu. Inexpensive.

◆◆
ANDHRÍTSAINA
(ANDHRITSENA)

western central Peloponnese
High in the Arcadian hills, Andhritsaina looks all too modern as you approach it, but once in among its narrow streets you discover it to be one of the loveliest of mountain villages. Traditional wooden houses have balconies overhanging the streets, and shops look as if they have not changed for centuries: the butcher, the baker, the cobbler, a tiny shop selling worry-beads. The old men sit, drink coffee and play cards, as they always have done.

Nearby

Along a winding mountain road, 14km south of Andhritsaina, is the Temple of Apollo at **Vassai** (**Bassae**). This wonderfully remote and well-preserved temple is covered by what appears to be an enormous circus tent, protecting it for restoration work. The site has open access.

◆◆◆
EPÍDHAVROS
(EPIDAURUS) ✓

southeast of Korinthos
The scent of the surrounding pine woods fills the air on the walk up from the entrance gate to the most beautiful Greek theatre in the world. Carved into the side of Mount Kynortio, Epidhavros is renowned for its acoustics: it is said that from the back of the 14,000-seat arena, with its 55 rows of seats, you can hear a pin drop on the stage far below. It is seldom

The world-famous theatre at Epidhavros

that this could be put to the test, because the site is immensely busy for much of the year, especially at weekends. Arrive early or late in the day, or out of season, if you hope for quiet rather than crowds.

The theatre was built in the 4th century BC and excavated in 1900 by archaeologists who had been working on the site since 1881. The whole area had been a place of pilgrimage for 200 years before the theatre even existed, as the sanctuary had been dedicated to the healing god Asclepius, son of Apollo. There were medical practitioners here, and patients who were healed made generous offerings. Such was its reputation that when Rome was struck by a plague in the 3rd century BC, the city sent for a serpent which was kept in the sanctuary here. A collection of medical instruments found on the site is on display in the museum, though the emphasis is more on its marvellous collection of statues. These

THE PELOPONNESE

range from the monumentally impressive to the finely delicate. Some reconstructed colonnades are especially grand. The museum is a long, narrow building, and the stonework lining the walls gives the rooms a sense of dignity. The archaeological site is still being worked on and, though many of the buildings are labelled, it still requires a feat of imagination for most visitors to see Epidhavros as it was. Most of the buildings are foundations only, with the remains of a stadium, a gymnasium and baths, added by the Romans and fed from the local curative springs. The site received sick visitors from all over Greece, like a modern spa. They would have stayed in rooms off the gymnasium, which was used as a banqueting hall. It can be rewarding to wander round these remnants, because most visitors come to see the theatre and, seeing what seems to be a

The harbour at Old Epidhavros

jumble of weeds and stones, ignore the rest.

The theatre is the star attraction, of course. A ring of flagstones marks the circular orchestra, in the centre of which is the small base of an altar. Around part of the edge runs a drainage channel, and between the two magnificent stone entrance arches is the stage itself. The foundations of this are clearly visible, when not covered by planks or scaffolding for a performance. Beyond the stage, the broad valley falls away to distant hills.

Now sympathetically restored, Epidhavros is a living theatre once again, a magnificent setting for classical drama and a key part of the Athens Festival. The works of ancient Greek dramatists such as Sophocles and Aristophanes are performed (in Greek) on weekend evenings from June until September. Exact times and days vary each year. Tickets are available at the site and in Athens, at the Drama

Festival box office (Odos Stadiou 4, tel: 322–1459).
Open: Monday to Friday 08.00–17.00hrs, Saturday and Sunday 08.30–15.00hrs.
Closed: public holidays.
Bus: Three daily from Navplion and two from Athens, direct to the site.

Accommodation
Xenia (tel: 0753–22003). This 26-room hotel in the grounds of Epidhavros offers an early start for exploring the site, but is booked well ahead for summer weekends. Some of the rooms are in stone bungalows hidden among the pines. Expensive.

◆◆◆
KALÁVRITA RAILWAY
southeast of Patrai
Every country has its Great Train Journey, and this is the one for Greece. The track runs for 22·5km from the small coastal resort of Dhiakofton, up through the Vouraikos Gorge to the mountain town of Kalavrita, 756m high.
The line was built by Italian engineers between 1885 and 1895 in order to bring minerals down from the mountains, and although the rolling stock has been modernised, the route itself remains as it was. The train sometimes pushes, sometimes pulls, and at other times needs help from a rack-and-pinion system to haul itself up the giddy gradients, sometimes as steep as 15 per cent. The track crosses the river several times on its way, disappears into tunnels and on occasion seems to hang in the air on narrow ledges overlooking the gorge, which itself is almost unbelievably narrow in places.
After almost an hour the train hauls itself into the mountain hamlet of Zahlorou, stopping briefly before the final stretch of the journey. The stop is actually called **Mega Spilio**, after the nearby monastery, said to be the oldest in Greece (though it has been burnt down and completely rebuilt several times).
Before reaching **Kalavrita** the gorge opens out and the route becomes pleasant rather than breathtaking. The Vouraikos river runs through Kalavrita, and above it looms Mount Velia. The clock on the tower in the church stands permanently at 2.34 – the time on 13 December 1943 when the Nazis, in a reprisal killing, slaughtered every male in the town over the age of 15. The death toll was 1,436.
The nearby **Monastery of Ayia Lavra** was also destroyed by the Germans, but has been rebuilt as a national shrine for it is also the place where the Greek War of Independence was declared in 1821. The town is thus a place of pilgrimage for many Greeks, and has a few hotels and tavernas, but the standard is basic and some visitors might prefer to have lunch here then catch the train for the awesome return journey back to the coast.
Open: all year. Several trains daily in each direction, with a journey time of about 70 minutes each way. For timetable details, tel: 01–513–1601.

THE PELOPONNESE

◆◆◆
KÓRINTHOS (CORINTH)

northeastern Peloponnese, west of Athens

Sandwiched between its famous canal and the fascinating site of Ancient Corinth, the modern town of Korinthos has little to offer visitors. Several earthquakes – most recently in 1928 and 1981 – have left their mark in a succession of drab, modern buildings. This is the centre for a thriving trade in one of Greece's main exports, the currant, which derives its name from the town.

Although the **Corinth Canal** is rivalled only by those at Panama and Suez for world renown, it is easy to miss this impressive feat of engineering. The bridge across it is an extremely busy highway, and other than the fact that the speed limit drops (in theory) to 20 kph, nothing announces that you are travelling over one of the wonders of the modern world. A café allows drivers to park and walk out across the walkway beside the road, vibrating from the passing juggernauts, to gaze down on the man-made channel of rock. The site of the city of **Ancient Corinth** lies 7km southwest of the modern town, and is much more interesting. The Romans made it the capital of their Greek province, displacing Athens. The site is marvellously atmospheric – the heart of a ruined town spread at your feet. At its height, in the 5th century BC, it had a population of 300,000, with a further 460,000 slaves. It also had a reputation

The Corinth Canal

The Emperor Nero first proposed a canal across the narrow isthmus here, to save ships a long journey round the whole of the Peloponnese. He is even said to have started the digging himself, with a golden shovel. He then left 6000 Jewish prisoners to get on with it, but the job was never finished. The project was only finally completed in 1893, after 12 years' work. Almost 6·5km long, with a dizzying drop of 90m, the canal is only 27m wide. This means that it cannot be used by today's supertankers and other large cargo ships, but some passenger ships and local vessels can still be seen plying the arrow-straight ribbon of water.

for licentious living – so St Paul's Epistles to the Corinthians were well aimed.

The museum, by the entrance gate, is rather disappointing, though there are some fine statue heads, and a large collection of vases. The most dominant of the surviving buildings, clearly visible as you approach the site, is the Temple of Apollo. This is one of the oldest temples in Greece, dating from the 6th century BC. If you stand here, with your back to the modern road, you will see the sprawling remains of the Roman market-place. Among these are several shops, some almost completely preserved, their walls and stone storage shelves intact. Large as it is, this is only the

lower town – a small part of what once was Corinth. Above, on a huge mass of rock, stands **Acrocorinth**, site of the town's acropolis. This is reached by a signposted road from the lower town. It is a journey well worth making, not least for the exhilarating drive, but to explore Acrocorinth in full you should allow an hour or two. The walls alone are 2km around. Inside them are other fortifications, as well as houses, mosques and churches. The views are quite stunning.
Open: lower town Monday to Friday 08.30–19.00hrs (17.00hrs in winter), Saturday and Sunday 08.00–15.00hrs; Acrocorinth Tuesday to Sunday 08.30–15.00hrs.

The Corinth Canal

Closed: public holidays.
Bus: 15 per day from Athens to modern Korinthos, connecting with a regular local service to Ancient Corinth (Arhea Korinthos).

◆◆
KORÓNI
on the coast southwest of Kalamai
Koroni is one of the most attractive small seaside resorts on the Messenian peninsula, to the west of the better-known Mani. Its narrow streets of whitewashed, balconied houses are as picturesque as those of any Greek island town with their blue and turquoise doors. Hidden away are little churches, and some fine old mansions with wrought-iron balconies, while above the town

THE PELOPONNESE

A tower house in the Mani

rises a 13th-century Venetian fortress, inside which are more houses and an attractive convent. A fine stretch of beach leads around a bay to the quieter neighbouring village of **Vasilitsi**. The attractive offshore island of **Venetiko** also has its own beach, easily reached on a boat trip from the harbour.

Accommodation
Hotel de la Plage, Vasilitsi (tel: 0725–22401). A small hotel with its own restaurant, half-hidden among olive groves and set in its own attractive grounds. Moderate.

Restaurant
Maistrali. One of the many waterfront tavernas and restaurants in Koroni. Particularly good Greek food, especially fish and meat from its charcoal grill.

♦♦♦
THE MANI ✓

south central Peloponnese
The Mani is the central peninsula of the three 'fingers' in the south of the Peloponnese. Its southernmost tip, Akra Tainaron (Cape Tenaro), was the mythical entrance to the underworld. This is the region of Mesa Mani (Deep Mani) – an area of rugged mountains and isolated villages with tall tower houses, and a part of Greece which seems to have changed little in the last hundred years. The northern half of the peninsula is Exo Mani (Outer Mani), with pleasant beach resorts and the dominating peaks of the Taiyetos mountain range rising to Profitis Ilias (2,404m). On the east coast is **Yithion** (or Gythion), the capital of the Mani – though situated more at its edge than at its heart. It is a small but bustling port, on the ferry routes between Athens and the islands of Kithira and Crete. Known as the octopus capital of Greece, Yithion's many inexpensive quayside tavernas (**Trata** is the best) feature this chewy but tasty delicacy and other very fresh fish. The waters here have always been rich in marine life: in Roman days there was a large export market in murex, a mollusc whose purple pigment was used to dye togas. Visitor attractions in Yithion are low-key to say the least, but the tall harbour-front buildings are attractive, as are the steep cobbled back-streets leading up to the old part of town. The main town for access to the

Tower Houses in the Mani

Many of the Mani's unique tower houses are being modernised and converted into guesthouses for visitors, in an enterprising government scheme to introduce a moderate amount of tourism. These houses were built to give the original owners the means of both attack and defence in the almost unbelievable blood feuds that dominated life in the Mani for 500 years from the 14th century onwards.

The feuds had stringent rules: all males from the enemy family were legitimate targets but the women could pass freely in and out of the houses and so bring in supplies. Hostilities ceased at harvest and certain other times, but otherwise the men would remain inside, sometimes for decades, with the aim of destroying not only their male enemies but the tower houses that belonged to them too. Roofs were particularly prized, so were prime targets for any missiles that could be hurled at them. As a protective measure the houses grew higher and higher, to four or five floors, still instantly identifying the Maniote landscape.

Mani in the west is **Kalamai** (**Kalamata**), the largest in the southern Peloponnese. A severe earthquake here in 1986 damaged the town badly, though today it has an increasingly busy airport and other facilities.

Head south down the coast to the attractive and lively village of **Kardhamili**, which is very busy in summer thanks to its splendid long stretch of pebbly beach. The old part of the village is also appealing, with abandoned tower houses and

the church of St Spyridon, which dates back to the 6th century.

As you head towards Deep Mani, there are three glorious sandy beaches at the resort of **Stoupa**, a very pleasant stopping place. The first truly typical Mani village is **Areopolis**, with narrow cobbled streets, tower houses and pleasant courtyards. It is also the main village for visiting

Fishing boats and ferries come and go in the harbour at Yithion

the bank, post office and garages.

A drive of about 12km south brings you to the **caves of Pirgos Dhirou**, one of the area's principal tourist attractions and very busy in summer (tel: 0733–52222). In high season, try to arrive early, and in any case buy your numbered ticket on arrival and do your waiting on the nearby beach or in the café. A boat takes you bumping along the underground river – naturally believed to be connected to the underworld – and through the 39 caves that have been exposed. The hundreds of stalactites, stalagmites and colourful rock formations are eerily beautiful. The caves are said to have been places of primitive worship in Neolithic and Paleolithic times, and were used as refuges by the resistance movement during World War II.

Another regular feature of the Mani landscape is the crumbling castles. A good example, near Mezapos, is the **Castle of Maina**, sometimes called Tigani ('frying pan') after the promontory on which it stands. Although dating from 1248, its ramparts in particular are still in a comparatively good state of preservation. It was built by William II de Villehardouin, the Frankish baron also responsible for the fine castles at Mistras and Monemvasia.

Among the best Mani villages dominated by clusters of tower houses are **Kita** and nearby **Boularioi**, in the south. It was in Kita that the last of the region's

blood feuds took place, as recently as 1870, when troops of soldiers had to be brought in to suppress the inter-family fighting. Now almost deserted, this was once the most powerful village in southern Mani, with more than 100 families and 22 tower houses. In Kato Boularioi, the lower half of this divided village, you can find one of the earliest surviving tower houses, the Anemodhoura tower, thought to date from 1600. The village also boasts around 20 churches, many with fine frescoes.

On the east coast, near the long, sandy beach of Vathi Bay, is the ruined **Castle of Passava**. Built in 1254, it complements the matching **Castle of Kelefa** in the west. The two together stand guard over the rugged region of Mesa Mani.

Most hotels and many restaurants in the Mani are closed in winter. The area is mainly geared to summer visitors, and out of season facilities can be hard to find.

Accommodation
Gythion, Odhos Emboros Vasilios Pavlo 33, Yithion (tel: 0733–22284). A smart 'A' class hotel right on the waterfront. Open all year. Moderate.
Pyrgos Kapetanakou, Areopolis (tel: 0733–51233). A small converted tower house. Its rooms are traditionally decorated, with four tower rooms and two ground-floor suites looking on to the flowered courtyard. Expensive.
Traditional Tower Hotels of Vathia (tel: 0733–54244). In the tiny village of Vathia, a remote

The huge theatre at Megalopolis remains largely unrestored

spot near the southern tip of the peninsula. Lovely traditional rooms, for those who really want to get away from it all. Expensive.

Tsitsiris Castle, Stavri (signposted off the main road south of Pirgos Dhirou; tel: 0733–54297). Sympathetically restored to provide 20 rooms, with traditional furniture but modern comforts. It also has a recommended cellar restaurant – see below. Expensive.

Restaurants

Lela's Taverna, Kardhamíli. A lively seafront eating place with a terrace overlooking the beach. Cheap. Immaculate and inexpensive rooms are also available. Open all year.

Tsitsiris Castle (see above): cellar restaurant. Though this resembles a western European wine bar, the food is recommended. You may find yourself eating in the company of the family who renovated the building. Open to non-residents. Moderate.

◆
MEGALÓPOLIS
central Peloponnese, southwest of Tripolis

Despite its name, Megalopolis is a small place but it is worth a visit for its ruined theatre, near by on the Andhritsaina road. Very little restoration work has been done, with only the first few rows of seats uncovered, but it is interesting to see this grass-covered arena in contrast to the splendours of restored theatres elsewhere, such as Delfi and Epidhavros. The theatre at Megalopolis was in fact the largest in ancient Greece, with seating for 20,000 people. Other, rather undistinguished ruins of ancient Megalopolis can be seen further on down the track.
Open: theatre at all times; other ruins daily 09.00–15.30hrs.

THE PELOPONNESE

◆◆
MESSÍNI (MESSENE)
*southwestern Peloponnese,
northwest of Kalamai*
A short footpath from the
attractive village of
Mavrommati leads to the ruins
of ancient Messini. It is said that
the city was built in 85 days, in
369 BC, as a new capital for this
region. The city walls are still
quite well preserved, and there
is also a small restored theatre
and the remains of temples and
the agora. The most outstanding
feature is the Arcadian Gate,
through which you will drive if
you head out of Mavrommati
towards Meligala. The
substantial gate has both outer
and inner entrances, separated
by a circular courtyard. A car is
essential, as Mavrommati has
no visitor facilities.
Open: ruins at all times.
Bus: two daily from Kalamai.

◆◆
METHÓNI
*extreme southwestern
Peloponnese*
Methoni's delightful streets are
lined with hundreds of red
hibiscus plants, while purple
bougainvillea and vivid blue
morning glories brighten the
houses and gardens. There is
an attractive large beach in the
centre of the town, but the
dominant feature is the huge
Venetian castle. This looks
impressive from the outside,
but is even more so inside the
walls, which seem to go on for
ever. There are ruined houses,
baths, and even the remains of
a cathedral – an atmospheric
place to wander.
Open: Monday to Saturday
08.30–15.00hrs, Sunday
09.00–15.00hrs.

Methoni: the harbour and bay

Accommodation

Methoni Beach (tel: 0723–31455). A hotel on the beach whose 13 large rooms all have private facilities. Only half-board bookings are taken in summer, but the restaurant is good and overlooks the beach. Moderate.

Restaurant

Taverna Klimateria. Here, just behind the Hotel Methoni Beach, is reputedly the best restaurant in the southern Peloponnese. Tables are in a quiet, walled garden, beneath spreading vines. The owners grow all their own vegetables, which enables them to offer an unusual variety of tasty vegetarian dishes. Closed in winter. Inexpensive.

◆◆
MIKÍNAI (MYCENAE)

south of Korinthos

The extraordinary German amateur archaeologist Heinrich Schliemann revolutionised accepted interpretations of Greek history by his excavations in the 1870s. Until then, the Homeric epics were widely assumed to have been fiction. Schliemann's discovery of Mycenae provided strong evidence that characters such as Agamemnon and his ill-fated family really did exist, and that this was their citadel.

The reputation of Ancient Mycenae as the focus of one of the most illustrious early civilisations is such that the reality of the site more than 3,000 years later can be disappointing. The magnificent treasures found here are in the Archaeological Museum in Athens, and you will need a vivid imagination to bring the site to life. But Mycenae is still well worth seeing, even though its ruins of a palace, houses, cisterns, a granary and a guardhouse are mostly little more than foundations.

On the approach from the modern village is a royal burial tomb, the Treasury of Atreus. This simple building, constructed without mortar, dates from about 1350BC and is the finest surviving beehive tomb. Its echoing acoustics amplify every footstep, every rustle of clothing. It is known as the Tomb of Agamemnon, but this remains speculation.

Further on, the site itself contains one of Ancient Greece's most familiar images: the Lion Gate. Over 7m high and dating from 1250BC, its 18-tonne lintel supports the famous carved lion relief. Its posts contain holes and sockets for doors and bars. Beyond is the Grave Circle marking the royal cemetery that Schliemann unearthed. A beautiful golden mask he found here caused him to send a cable to the King of Greece announcing 'I have gazed upon the face of Agamemnon.' Such a stirring statement deserves to be true, even if the evidence suggests that Schliemann's finds were from the very early Mycenean age, some 300 years before Agamemnon and the Trojan War.

Open: Monday to Friday 08.00–17.00hrs, Saturday and Sunday 08.30–15.00hrs.
Closed: public holidays.
Bus: three daily from Korinthos and Navplion.

THE PELOPONNESE

Accommodation

La Belle Helene, in modern Mikinai's single main street, Odhos Tsounta (tel: 0751–66255). This was Schliemann's own house. His room, number 3, looks towards the ruins, and the impressive visitors' book includes the signatures of Virginia Woolf, Debussy and Henry Moore. Inexpensive.

Restaurant

Achilleus, Odhos Tsounta (tel: 0751–66027). Friendly service and good home cooking make this the best. Inexpensive.

◆◆◆
MISTRAS (MYSTRA)
west of Sparti

Not as well known as many older sites, Mistras should nevertheless be on everyone's itinerary. This walled Byzantine city, once home to 45,000 people but now crumbling and almost deserted, straddles paths that zig-zag up a flower-filled hillside, topped by a splendid Frankish castle. Entering Mistras is like stepping into a film set or a dream world. Buy a guide with a map at either of the two entrances – the upper one gives easier access to the castle, which is otherwise a tiring climb.

The castle was built in 1249 by William II de Villehardouin, while most of the buildings huddling below it for protection are from the 14th and 15th centuries. They include the Cathedral, dedicated to Ayios Dhimitrios, whose torture and death are vividly portrayed in one of the church's many detailed frescoes. Elsewhere in

Heinrich Schliemann

A German businessman reared on stories from Homer might seem an unlikely person to change the face of Greek archaeology, but Heinrich Schliemann (1822–90) did just that.

While busy making his fortune on both sides of the Atlantic, Schliemann never forgot the impact that tales of Ancient Greece had on him as a boy. He retired from commerce as soon as possible and, to the horror of the scholarly establishment, began to investigate Ancient Greece with a spade. His first coup, in 1870, was the discovery of the site of Troy at Hissarlik. Not content with this, he began to dig at Mycenae, with spectacular results.

The professionals could no longer ignore Schliemann's work: archaeologists from all over the world began piecing together a picture of Mycenean culture. But without Schliemann, the existence of this great early civilisation would have remained, at most, guesswork.

the jumble of streets are the remnants of once-splendid mansions, mosques, churches and monasteries. The Pantanassa Convent is still inhabited by nuns, its courtyard a mass of flowers, its church the finest in Mistras. The Perivleptos Monastery stands empty, but the echoing walls of its church are decorated with some delightful frescoes. One of the best surviving buildings

is the Despot's Palace, though this is likely to be inaccessible for some years because of lengthy restoration work.
Open: Tuesday to Sunday 08.30–15.00hrs.
Closed: public holidays.
Bus: sporadic service from Sparti to modern Mistras, leaving a long uphill walk to the lower entrance of old Mistras.

Accommodation
Byzantio (tel: 0731–93309). On the Sparti road in new Mistras is its only hotel, with rather ordinary but clean rooms. Moderate.

Restaurant
Grill House Mistras, main square. Looks very ordinary (as a Greek taverna should) but serves excellent food, especially grilled meat dishes. Cheap.
To Kastro (opposite the hotel). Good but expensive.

MONEMVASÍA
southeastern Peloponnese, on the east coast
There are two Monemvasias, one the small modern port town, the other the invisible old Monemvasia. This is a 13th-century Byzantine town, concealed at the back of the enormous rock that is not surprisingly known as the Gibraltar of Greece. It first looms into view some distance away along the coastal roads, but even from the causeway that connects the rock to the mainland nothing can be seen of the secret medieval settlement which faces the sea on the far side.
Cars are left at the entrance: access to the walled town is through a gateway wide enough only for one man and

The Frankish castle at Mistras

THE PELOPONNESE

his loaded donkey. The name Monemvasia derives from this 'single entrance', or *Moni Emvasis*. The defences were such that Monemvasia held an important strategic position and seldom fell to invaders. It was only after a three-year siege that William II de Villehardouin captured it in 1249.

Today the old town has a permanent population of only about 50, though this is swollen by the tourist trade with tavernas, rooms, shops and a couple of hotels tucked into narrow alleyways. Flowers of every colour peek through holes in derelict buildings, and from pots outside those houses still occupied. There are several churches worth visiting, including the cathedral which dates from the end of the 13th century. In the modern town are facilities such as banks, ticket agencies, a post office and a number of tavernas and small hotels. Accommodation on the rock is restricted.

Accommodation
Byzantio (tel: 0732–61351).
Malvasia (tel: 0732–61323).
These two 'hotels' in the main street of the old town spread across several restored houses. Some of the rooms have marbled bathrooms and rug-covered floors. Expensive.

Restaurants
Estiatorio Matoula (main street). Traditional Greek menu. Fine views out to sea from the rear: a splendid setting for a leisurely evening meal. Moderate.
To Kanoni (main street). Specialises in fish. Moderate.

◆◆◆
NÁVPLION ✓

south of Korinthos
One of the most delightful towns in mainland Greece, Navplion stands under a walled fortress and looks across a huge bay to the distant Arcadian hills. With good hotels, excellent food and easy access to beaches and classical sites, it makes the perfect base. A limestone hill to the northwest bears the ruins of the ancient citadel of **Tiryns**, impressive for its massive, thick walls more than 3,000 years old. Navplion's old houses cluster under the fortress of **Palamidhi**, accessible either by road or by a tiring climb up almost 1,000 steps. Inside the walls are three Venetian castles built between 1711 and 1714 – not to be confused with the nearby Its Kale ('Three Castles') fortress, which is crumbling and offers much less to see.

The **archaeological museum**, in Platia Sindagma, has two floors of well-displayed exhibits, including a marvellous suit of Mycenean armour (tel: 0752–27502). The award-winning **folklore museum** at the junction of Ipsilandhrou and Sofroni should not be missed. Its fine displays of traditional Greek clothing, household artefacts, looms and old photographs are complemented by an excellent shop selling handicrafts (tel: 0752–28379).

Nearby

The beach resort of **Tolon**, with water-sports and nightlife, is 12km to the south, while history-lovers can make easy day-trips to Epidhavros, Mikinai and Korinthos.

Accommodation

King Otto, Odhos Farmakopoulou 2 (tel: 0752–27585). The best inexpensive hotel, housed in an old mansion. Breakfast is served in its scented garden. Closed in winter.
Xenia, Close to the Xenia Palace, and equally pleasant if not quite as plush. Moderate.
Xenia Palace, in the lower part of Its Kale (tel: 0752–28981). Inside is wood and marbled elegance, outside glorious views. Expensive.

Restaurants

Estiatorio Kakanarakis, Vassilisis Olgas 18. Changing daily specials, and wine ranging from expensive to straight-from-the-barrel. Moderate.
O Arapakos, on the waterfront at Bouboulinas 81. The best Greek cooking. Try an oven-baked dish, such as *youvetsi ton arapi* (beef with potatoes, tomatoes, carrots and aubergines, topped with cheese and cooked in a clay pot). Moderate.

Navplion's sheltered bay and busy waterfront

THE PELOPONNESE

◆◆◆
OLIMBÍA (OLYMPIA) ✓

western Peloponnese, east of Pirgos

Even the most jaded visitor, suffering from a surfeit of classical sites, could not fail to be moved by walking down the contestants' entrance to the original Olympic stadium. The tunnel leads out to the running track, where the starting and finishing lines can still be seen. Here the Olympic flame begins its journey, having been lit from the sun's rays in the ruins of the nearby Temple of Hera.

Buy a detailed guidebook to help you make sense of the jumble of buildings, such as the Temples of Zeus and Hera, the Sacred Precinct, the studio of the sculptor Pheidias, the Fountain House and many more relics of this ancient Olympic village. The **museum** justifies its separate entrance fee with one of the best sculpture collections outside Athens.

Open: Monday to Friday 08.00–19.00hrs, Saturday and Sunday 09.00–15.00hrs.
Closed: public holidays.
Bus: three daily from Athens, hourly from Pirgos.

The site is a short walk from the modern village of **Olimbía,** which is little more than a single street of souvenir shops, cafés and hotels for the tourist trade, but it has a pleasant, lively atmosphere. The **Olympic Games Museum** has an entertaining history of the modern Games.

Open: Monday to Saturday 08.00–15.30hrs, Sunday 09.00–16.30hrs.

The Olympic Games
Games were held at Olympia long before 776BC, but that date marks the beginning of the official four-yearly Olympiad. Competitors from all the Greek city-states took part in contests ranging from chariot races to poetry and music, as well as events more familiar today such as sprinting and discus.

The Games were banned in AD393 by new legislation to control pagan celebrations. Their site decayed and was eventually forgotten and buried by silt.

Some 15 centuries passed before the site was excavated. The Games were re-born in 1896, and the International Olympic Academy still controls the Games from its base at Olimbía.

Accommodation
New Apollon, Douma 13 (tel: 0624–22513/22522). Recommended for its comfortable rooms and rooftop swimming pool. Moderate.
Xenia, Odhos Praxitelous (tel: 0624–22510). Peaceful, and a short walk away from the ancient site. Moderate.

Restaurant
Taverna Praxitelis, Odhos Spiliopoulou 7 (tel: 0624–22592). Immaculately decorated, with pine walls and fresh flowers. Greek dishes such as *stifado* (beef stew), and quail when in season, feature on the menu and portions are very generous. Moderate.

◆
SPÁRTI (SPARTA)
south central Peloponnese, south of Tripolis

Do not expect to see too much of Sparta's illustrious past in the large, modern town that now exists here. It is enjoyable and lively, but a one-night stay should be enough for most visitors.

Remains are scattered around the modern town, the main cluster being to the north. Here are the skeletal remains of a large theatre, the foundations of a Temple to Athena and the hill on which the acropolis stood, now occupied by a Byzantine church and a small monastery. Relics from the surrounding area are housed in the **archaeological museum** (tel: 0731–28575) on Odhos Dhionysos Dhafnou. The collection is small but, in the

The track at Olympia. Athletes competed here 2,800 years ago

absence of grand ruins, worth seeing, and the museum itself has a relaxing statue-filled garden.
Open: Tuesday to Sunday 08.30–15.00hrs.
Another attraction is an extremely busy **market** on Wednesday and Saturday mornings, in and around the pedestrianised Kleomvrotoa shopping area.

Accommodation
Maniatis, Odhos Paleologou 72 (tel: 0731–22665). A large, modern, central hotel, much better than its 'C' rating might suggest. Moderate.

An Ancient State
Sparta was founded in the 9th century BC under rules laid down by a legislator named Lycurgus. He united four villages in this fertile plain, dividing the population into three classes, under two kings and a single senate. The experiment was successful and the state flourished to such an extent that Sparta defeated Athens after the 30-year Peloponnesian War. Victory was short-lived, however, as the war had taken many of Sparta's men and resources, and from the 6th century BC life in Sparta was austere... hence, 'spartan'.

Restaurant
Elysse, Odhos Paleologou 113 (tel: 0731–23630). Looks more French than Greek but is one of the few places serving Spartan specialities. *Kotopoulo bardouniotiko* is delicious – chicken sautéed with onions and potatoes and topped with a slab of feta cheese. Moderate.

◆
YERAKI
southeastern Peloponnese, southeast of Sparti
The remoteness of Yeraki (or Geraki) discourages many visitors, but its fine setting rewards dedicated enthusiasts who manage to reach it. The modern hill village is much smaller than its important Byzantine predecessor. Its narrow streets are daunting for drivers – the 'main' road snakes among the houses like a roller-coaster, and even the village square is on two levels. Fortunately, Yeraki is served by several buses daily from Sparti.

To the southeast stands the Frankish castle of medieval Yeraki, built in 1254 on the slopes of Mount Parnon and offering superb views of the surrounding plains and mountains. Inside are old cisterns, and the church of Ayios Yiorgos. The castle is surrounded by no fewer than 15 chapels. These are normally locked, but any visitor showing a flicker of interest in the café on the village's main square will be offered either the keys or even a guided tour by the caretaker. The site is approached by a very bad road, so is easier to reach on foot: allow a couple of hours.

The fragmentary remains of Sparta's once immense amphitheatre

Peace and Quiet

Countryside and Wildlife in Mainland Greece by Paul Sterry

Few holiday destinations can rival Greece for its combination of human history and natural history interest. Archaeological sites abound, and these are often excellent for wildlife: planted trees provide shade for birds, and ruins are home to numerous lizards and insects. Add to this the prospect of extensive mountain ranges, scrub-covered hillsides and wetland areas and you have a perfect destination for anyone with even a passing interest in wild creatures and plants. Much of mainland Greece is mountainous. The difficult terrain means that many areas are inaccessible except on foot. However, this does mean that visitors who are prepared to walk off the beaten track can easily escape the crowds, even in high season. Although most of the native woodland has been felled, you will find scrub-covered hillsides full of flowers and home to many species of insects and small birds. The coastline is also extremely rewarding, with dramatic cliffs, extensive river deltas, marshlands and salt-pans. The general 'feel' of the coastal

landscape is typically Mediterranean. Where native pine forests once reached down to the sea, visitors are now likely to find small fields, olive groves, orchards or vineyards. Although heavily influenced by man, all the coastal habitats hold wildlife surprises.

One of the great glories of a spring visit to Greece is the colourful flowers. In common with the Mediterranean region as a whole, many plants here do most of their growing during the wet autumn and winter, flower in the spring and then wither in the parched heat of summer. Wild orchids are abundant in many places, as are irises, gladioli, vetches,

---

Some Birds of the Coast
black-throated diver
(Oct–Apr)
Cory's shearwater
Manx shearwater
shag
Kentish plover
Mediterranean gull
black-headed gull (Oct–Apr)
lesser black-backed gull
herring gull

PEACE AND QUIET

cistuses and many more.
Botanists often use the altitude
to their advantage when
hunting for flowers. If you come
here after the best flowering
period – April to June – simply
climb higher to find plants
whose flowering has been
delayed by the lingering snows.
Mainland Greece is on an
important route for many
migrant birds which return to
northern Europe each spring
from south of the
Mediterranean in order to
breed; they pass through the
region in their hundreds of
thousands each spring and
autumn. In fact, many of
Greece's characteristic
Mediterranean species are only
summer visitors, arriving in
April and May and departing
again in the autumn for Africa.
Northeastern Greece perhaps
offers the best birdwatching on
the mainland, but the coastal
lagoons and wetlands around
Arta and Mesolongion in the
west are worth visiting, and the
numerous small ports of the
eastern Peloponnese are good
places to search for seabirds,
including unusual gulls. Late
winter and early spring are the
best times.
The following pages briefly
describe a few of the best
wildlife areas on the Greek
mainland.

Angelokhorion
*Salt-pans and coastal peninsula
near Thessaloniki.*
Angelokhorion lies due south of
Thessaloniki, not far from the
international airport. Take the
main road southeast from the
city towards Arnaia and turn off

> ### Wild Orchids
> Many species of orchid thrive
> in the hot summers and mild,
> wet winters of the eastern
> Mediterranean. A large
> number of orchids also prefer
> limey soils. Greece has both
> the climate and the geology to
> suit these fascinating and
> beautiful flowers, and finding
> the many different kinds can
> be among the chief pleasures
> of a stay here.
> From the northerly mountains
> of Makedhonia to the warmer
> slopes of the Mani in the
> southern Peloponnese,
> mainland Greece offers
> conditions to suit many rare,
> and even more of the
> commoner, orchid species.
> February is not too soon to
> look for some varieties such
> as the aptly named giant
> orchid (*Barlia*) or certain early
> types of bee orchid in the
> warm south, while even as late
> as July, north-facing slopes
> high in the mountains may still
> be good places to hunt for
> some of the helleborine
> species, particularly the
> unusually handsome red
> helleborine.

south near the airport to Ayia
Trias. Drive through the rather
run-down holiday town and
continue until the minor road
peters out near the sea.
In spring and autumn, the salt-
pans here are alive with gulls.
In particular, look for white-
winged Mediterranean gulls as
well as rarer species such as
slender-billed and Audouin's
gulls. Search the various pools
and salt-pans to find a large

selection of waders and terns.
Larks and wagtails are
numerous in the short grass
close to the sea, where tortoises
and Balkan wall lizards are also
abundant. Look, too, for shells
on the beach – the beautiful
murex is often found. During
periods of strong onshore
winds, Cory's shearwaters fly
by close to the beach. On a
clear day, there is a stunning
backdrop of Mount Olimbos
(Olympos) across the
Thermaïkos Kolpos (Thermaic
Gulf).

Ávas Gorge

*Dramatic gorge, some 20km
north of Alexandhroupolis, good
for birds of prey.*
To reach the Ávas Gorge, drive
north on the minor road from
Alexandhroupolis which goes
through Ávas village and ends
at Aisimi.
The road passes through the
gorge itself. Stop and scan the
skies and the rock faces. Blue
rock-thrushes sing from rocky
outcrops and subalpine
warblers skulk in the
undergrowth, but it is for birds
of prey that Ávas is most
famous. It would not be unusual
to see six or seven species in a
few hours; these might include
Egyptian vulture, buzzard,
short-toed eagle and lanner
falcon.
In spring and autumn, migrant
birds of prey fly through the
gorge and flocks of white storks
and pelicans are also seen. At
these times of year, it is worth

*White storks (and visitors) in their
lofty home*

PEACE AND QUIET

stopping on your way back to the coast to look in the olive groves beside the road. Colourful flowers and butterflies abound, and smaller migrant birds such as masked shrikes and collared flycatchers can also be found.

Delfí (Delphi)

Famous and spectacular archaeological site (see pages 56–8), one of the best places in Greece to observe mountain birds.

Delfí is perhaps the most dramatic of all archaeological sites in mainland Greece. It lies in a ravine with a view overlooking the Pleistos valley some 700m below. Many of the

Ancient sites like Delfi are not just for history buffs. They are also good for spotting wildlife

temples and other remains have been restored and trails, some of them steep and arduous, lead among them. These paths are good for anyone keen to discover some of the mountain wildlife of Greece.

One of the first birds you will notice is the rock nuthatch, which actively searches for food among the ruins. Hoopoes, unmistakable with their black-tipped crests, also live around the site. Cretzschmar's buntings and Ruppell's warblers are specialities of the scrub-covered hillsides, where a wide variety of songbirds can be found among the trees and bushes in spring and early summer. Early mornings are best for these birds, before the sun gets too hot. Lizards dart among the ruins, and praying mantids are common.

Delfi is also good for birds of prey including Egyptian and griffon vultures, golden eagles and lanner falcons. The longer you spend at Delfi, the better your chances of seeing a good variety of raptors.

April and May are the best months for flowers. Among the junipers and tree heathers, look for cistuses, vetches, irises and orchids.

Kalávrita Forest

Protected area around Kalavrita in the northern Peloponnese.
This little-known but beautiful area covers more than 1,700 hectares and is well worth visiting. In spring there are colourful flowers, such as cistuses and tree heathers, to be found. Small birds such as Orphean warblers, serins and firecrests sing from the cover of the undergrowth while, as in many remote and mountainous areas of Greece, birds of prey wheel overhead, becoming more common with increasing elevation.

Kavála and the Néstos Delta

The attractive port of Kavala is a good base for exploring the Nestos delta to the east.
Gulls and other seabirds can usually be seen around the coast at Kavala, and the skies are full of pallid swifts and red-rumped swallows in spring and summer. To reach the Nestos delta, drive east from Kavala and turn south on a minor road at Gravouna that leads to Khrisokhori and eventually to the port of Keramoti. Just north of Keramoti there are lagoons on the east side of the road: look here for waders, herons, terns, gulls and the occasional flock of flamingos. Another road runs north, on the outskirts of Keramoti, to Pegai. Here you can cross the river and walk along the banks, looking for wildlife.

Ancient Sites in the Peloponnese

Sites such as Mycenae, Corinth, Epidhavros and Olympia harbour plenty of wildlife interest as well as antiquities. Bare, trampled ground around the ruins is often surprisingly good for spring orchids. Sometimes, unfortunately, the ground immediately around the ruins is sprayed with weedkillers, but if you wander even a short distance away from the main site you will seldom be disappointed. Though most of the orchids may be over by late spring, they are followed by other delights such as masses of colourful poppies, and at any time of year there are the typical Mediterranean aromatic shrubs, such as thyme, myrtle, juniper and lavender, to enjoy. Lizards bask on rocks and walls, and the monuments themselves are often home to rock nuthatches, which call loudly in the spring.

PEACE AND QUIET

Kóronia, Límni (Lake Koronia)

Large, reed-fringed lake a short distance northeast of Thessaloniki.

To reach Lake Koronia, take the E90 out of Thessaloniki and shortly turn off north to the village of Agios Vassilios (the lake is also known as Lake Vassilios) and the southern shores of the lake. The many untidy-looking nests in the village – some on telegraph poles and others on the roofs of houses – belong to white storks. These huge nests also attract other birds: look for house sparrows, tree sparrows and Spanish sparrows nesting among the tangled twigs and branches.

Spring is the best season to visit the lake. Birdwatchers should look for pelicans, herons, egrets and waders. Frogs are abundant along the shoreline and provide meals for many of the birds.

Mesolóngion (Missolonghi)

A coastal site in the west, good for wetland birds.

Mesolongion lies on the west coast of the mainland, on the shores of an immense lagoon. Although this in itself makes it good for coastal birds, the presence of large numbers of fish hatcheries and salt-pans increases its appeal to many wild creatures. The lagoons and hatcheries along the shorelines can be seen from the road, but ask permission of the owners if you want to explore further.

In the spring, avocets and black-winged stilts nest on the banks of the lagoons and channels, while migrant waders stop off to feed along the water's edge. Terns and gulls are also present in good numbers and dry areas of land have breeding Kentish plovers, stone curlews and short-toed larks.

Mikri Prespa, Limni (Lake Mikri-Prespa National Park)

Large lake with reed-bed margins straddling the border between Greece and Albania.

Access is poor, but a minor road runs around the northern perimeter of the lake. Turn off the main road between Kastoria and Florina roughly 35km north of Kastoria and 30km west of Florina.

Lake Mikri-Prespa is best known as a haunt of breeding wetland birds and, in particular, specialities of the region such as Dalmatian pelicans and pygmy cormorants. Views of these and other birds such as herons, egrets and ibises will be distant, but if you scan the reed-beds, you should be able to see most species. The road between Kastoria and Florina passes through some excellent areas of beech wood. Interesting flowers grow in the dark shade, including several species of orchid. Fungi are abundant in autumn and woodland birds can be seen too.

Ólimbos (Olympos) National Park

The highest mountain in Greece; a good place to see mountain birds and wild flowers.

PEACE AND QUIET

*A fertile, well-watered plain
separates Olympos from the sea*

This limestone mountain range
is largely inaccessible, but two
suggested routes are as
follows. Firstly, the road which
runs to the south of the highest
point, Mitikas (2,917m), from
Skala Leptokaria on the coast
through Kari to Kallithea
Olimbou, is worth exploring.
Secondly, driving along the
Litokhoron road to Prionia in the
Enipefs valley allows you to
explore the magnificent forests
of black pine as well as above
the tree-line. A good range of
mountain species can be found.
More than 1,500 species of
plant grow on Olympos.
Around 20 of these are found
nowhere else in the world. The
list is long but species of gentian,
buttercup, cistus, saxifrage,
fritillary and orchid are all easy
to find. The birdlife ranges from
typically woodland species in
the pine forest – crested tits,
firecrests and woodpeckers –
to mountain species including
rock partridges, ortolan
buntings and alpine accentors
above the tree-line.

Párnis Óros (Mount Parnes) National Park
*Extensive mountain range with
gorges and limestone flora, less
than 40km northwest of Athens.*
Take the minor road north from
Akharnai in the west of the city.
The road runs high into the
mountains and not far from the
highest point in the range, at
1,413m. Stop from time to time
to explore the landscape
beside the road.
The mountain range, roughly
40km long, is partly cloaked in
woodland. There are oaks as
well as Greek firs and aleppo
pines. There are also areas of
maquis (Mediterranean scrub
woodland) comprising kermes
oaks, strawberry trees and
many others. The ground flora
is colourful in the spring with
cistuses, tree heathers and
orchids, while birdlife includes

PEACE AND QUIET

several species of warblers and cirl buntings. Look for praying mantids and butterflies.

Parnassós Óros (Mount Parnassos) National Park
Dramatic mountain scenery roughly 150km west of Athens, with access to areas above the tree-line.
Drive to Arakhova and then turn off north to Lilea. The range is close to Delfi, making a combined visit well worth considering. The skiing centre car park, off the Arakhova – Lilea road, is a good starting point.
In the forests you can expect to see woodland birds such as crested tits, firecrests and black woodpeckers, while above the tree-line, alpine accentors, ortolan buntings, rock thrushes and black redstarts are among the attractions. Always keep an eye on the skies for birds of prey such as griffon vultures and golden eagles.
The slopes of the Parnassos range are an excellent place to look for wild flowers in spring and summer: narcissi, crocuses, gentians and orchids grow almost everywhere.

Pórto Lágo
Wetland area between Xanthi and Komotini – home to waterbirds in abundance.
Park at the village of Porto Lago, close to the E5 on the coast, east of Xanthi and near to the southern end of Limni Vistonis (Lake Vistonia). Salt-pans and a lagoon lie on the coastal side of the road; walk out along the causeway to the church of St Nikolaos,

Water margins and reed-beds are likely places to see a tree frog

surrounded by water. Scan the water and reed-beds for Mediterranean and slender-billed gulls, glossy ibises, pygmy cormorants and many more. On the northern side of the road is Lake Mpourou, with Lake Vistonia beyond. This is also good for birds such as herons, egrets and terns.

Practical

*This section (with the
yellow band) includes food,
drink, shopping,
accommodation, nightlife,
tight budget, special
events etc.*

FOOD AND DRINK

While Greece does not have
one of the great cuisines of the
world, eating out can be one of
the highlights of any visit.
Dining Greek-style does have
something unique: its
atmosphere.
A meal might be anything from
a simple omelette rustled up in
the only café in some remote
village to a multi-course meal in
a top-notch Athens restaurant
where the food (and the bill)
will rival any other European
capital.
Most Greek meals are taken in
that great Greek invention, the
taverna, or the slightly more up-
market *estiatorio* (restaurant).
The difference between the two
can sometimes be no more than
the name, but *estiatoria* (in the
plural) are found more often in
towns and cities, tavernas in
villages and beach resorts.
Many tavernas are family affairs
– perhaps with grandmother
sitting in the corner peeling
potatoes and the youngest of
children acting very maturely
as waiters. The Greeks love
children, and this also applies to
mealtimes. Meals are family

Peppers drying in the sun

occasions, and children dine
with their families until late at
night.

Eating Habits

Greeks eat late, perhaps not
until 14.00hrs for lunch and
21.00hrs for dinner, although
eating places open much
earlier. The cooking is done
early, however, with the result
that some dishes can be
lukewarm by the time they are
eaten. This should not be cause
for complaint, but is simply the
Greek way. If you like your

FOOD AND DRINK

Aubergines and tomatoes are staple ingredients of many Greek dishes

food hot, choose a grill or fresh fish rather than *moussaka*, which will have been prepared in advance.

Telephone numbers of restaurants listed in this book are only given where you might need them, in Athens or for very popular local restaurants. Except for smart city restaurants it is seldom necessary to reserve a table. The Greek approach is to turn up, often in enormous numbers, at the busiest time, and expect to be seated. Restaurant-owners are usually equal to this, dragging extra tables and chairs in from somewhere. If a place is full, wait and look hopeful.

Most menus show two prices side by side, with and without tax. You pay the higher, but both must be shown by law. Prices are controlled by the tourist police, and should be openly displayed. Menus are often in English and Greek, but it is normal to ask to see the day's dishes in the kitchen. You cannot judge a Greek eating place by looks, unless it shows obvious signs of neglect. The most basic places often serve the most wonderful food. Watch where the locals eat.

A Greek meal can be a rather unpredictable sequence of courses. Dishes come when they are ready, so a side-order of salad or fried potatoes may arrive at the start of a meal, the main dish 20 minutes later. If you cannot adjust to this way of eating, you will have to adjust your ordering habits, requesting things when you want them.

What to Order

Mezedes or *meze* is a good way to begin. It comprises a selection of 'starters', often large enough for a complete meal. They may include familiar dishes such as *taramosalata* (cod's roe paté), *tzatziki* (yoghourt, garlic and cucumber dip) and *melitzanosalata* (aubergine paté).

Fish is popular but expensive. It is sold by weight so choose the piece you want, asking for it to be weighed and priced beforehand. Greeks have big appetites, so if you ask for a swordfish steak you may get an enormous and pricey portion. Swordfish (*xifias*) is common and delicious, as is fried squid (*kalamari/kalamarakia*). Other typical fish dishes are red mullet (*barbouni*), lobster (*astakos*) and whitebait (*marides*).

Fish and meat are cooked on the charcoal grill in many tavernas. Try chicken (*kotopoulo*), lamb (*arni*) or pork (*hirino*), any of which can be served as *souvlaki*: skewered chunks, with or without pieces of tomato, onion and pepper. Vegetarianism is not common, but most menus offer a limited choice of suitable dishes. Anything stuffed (tomatoes, peppers, aubergines, vine leaves) may or may not have minced meat in, so ask. Otherwise there are *gigandes* (white beans), *koukia* (broad beans), *vriam* (ratatouille), *voureki* (courgette,potato and cheese pie) and a variety of vegetable salads including *horiatiki* (Greek salad). Desserts are limited, sticky and sweet, such as *baklava* (honey and nuts in pastry), *galaktoboureko* (custard pie) and *kataifi* (shredded wheat soaked in honey). These are often eaten at a *zaharoplasteion* (patisserie), with a Metaxa brandy, though tourist restaurants may have a small dessert menu and most will offer some kind of fruit, frequently watermelon (*karpouzi*).

Drinks
Greek wine (*krasi*) has even less of an international reputation than Greek cooking. *Aspro* is white, *mavro* red, *sero* dry and *gliko* sweet. Retsina is a unique Greek white wine, with a heavy pine resin flavour from the barrels in which it was stored. It is not to everyone's taste, but complements the oil-rich Greek food very well.

Fast food in the Plaka

SHOPPING

Souvenir shops offer the usual knick-knacks, with a heavy emphasis on ceramics. By looking around, it is possible to find more unusual items from craftsmen rather than mass-produced goods. Leather is a good buy, from purses to coats. Woollen blankets are easily found, along with sheepskin rugs (*flokati*), particularly nearer Turkey.

Among the best buys are gold and silver jewellery, for which the Greeks have a reputation, notably in Athens and Ioannina. There are exquisite rings, earrings and necklaces to be bought. Other delicate work is seen in embroidery and hand-woven items, lace, cotton skirts and blouses.

Many towns have folk museums of traditional clothing and

Greek jewellery can be a good buy

decorative work. Often there will be a museum shop selling modern examples. If not, enquire where local specialists can be found.

Tapes of Greek music are good souvenirs, and worry-beads are found hanging in most tourist shops. Many kinds of Greek food and wine tend not to travel well, but some brand-name spirits are good bargains, and cooks can stock up on cheap virgin olive oil.

Haggling is acceptable in certain circumstances, notably in tourist areas such as the Plaka in Athens. Here shop-owners will start you off on the process anyway by immediately quoting you a price less than the one on the ticket. A gullible purchaser may accept this as a bargain, rather than wondering if the price might come down further. It usually will. Jewellery and craft shops often have room for manoeuvre, although by no means as much as is common in eastern or North African countries.

A junk shop in Monastiraki

ACCOMMODATION

Accommodation is inspected regularly by the Tourist Police and graded according to a range of criteria. These grades are a guide, not a guarantee of quality. For example, large rooms will tend to have a higher grading than small ones, irrespective of furnishings. Hotel grades run from Luxury to 'E' class, Luxury being the only grade for which there is no set price scale. These will be on a par with luxury hotels anywhere in the world. 'A' and 'B' class generally have most or all of their rooms with private facilities, 'C' class hotels can be anything, while 'D' and 'E' class would not have private facilities and would be budget options. Room prices should by law be displayed on a notice in the room, and you can check against the rate you are asked to pay. Rates change according to season; prices can be quoted with and without taxes, or with and without breakfast. Early in the season the previous year's notice may still be on display. All these can account for slight discrepancies, but in the unlikely event of your being badly overcharged, report the matter to the Tourist Police. Prices are generally quoted per room rather than per person. Where single rooms are unavailable a double room may be offered at a reduced rate. Because standards vary, ask to see a room before committing yourself. Foreign visitors must surrender their passports to enable the owner to complete necessary records.

If you are travelling outside the busy seasons of Easter and August, you should not need to book accommodation, but bear in mind that many large hotels in tourist resorts close out of season.

Rooms to rent (*Domatia*)

In tourist resorts you will see signs saying 'Rooms to rent', '*Zimmer Frei*' or '*Domatia*'. Accommodation of this kind ranges from self-contained apartments to a simple room in someone's house, where you may find yourself living alongside the family. Rooms will usually be clean, and visitors will be given a warm welcome. Prices here are more negotiable.

Like most ports, Yithion in the Mani has a range of places to eat

CULTURE, ENTERTAINMENT AND NIGHTLIFE

A typically Greek evening's entertainment will involve a lengthy meal, followed by music and dancing. In tourist areas such as the Plaka in Athens, tavernas sometimes offer entertainment of some kind in summer. Perhaps there will be strolling musicians, or perhaps the waiters will down trays and dance, picking up tables with their teeth or some such favourite (and impressive) Greek party-piece.

If you prefer more sophisticated entertainment, the events to watch out for are those of the annual Athens Festival, from June to September. There are concerts, both modern and classical, and plenty of drama, with performances of plays by Sophocles, Euripedes and other classical dramatists very much to the fore. These take place mainly at the Odeon of Herod Atticus below the Akropolis (see page 34), but also at weekends at Epidhavros (see pages 70-3). Transport from Athens is organised to coincide with the productions. Greek National Tourist Organisations abroad can provide a programme, as can most hotels and travel operators in Greece. To book, contact the Festival Box Office, Stadhiou 4, Athens (tel: 01–322–1459/322–3111), open from Monday to Friday, 08.30–13.30hrs and 18.00–20.30hrs. Tickets can also be bought at event venues. To find out about other events in Athens, see

Media, page 116.

Thessaloniki has an October arts festival, and there are often performances in some of the ancient theatres such as those at Dhion (page 45), Dhodhoni (page 58) and Filippi (page 46). Check locally, or obtain the annual Greek Festivals leaflet from the GNTO.

For the rest, Greek people welcome any excuse for making their own entertainment. Instead of birthdays they celebrate name days, when people bearing the same first name celebrate together. These will include services at churches of that name and, in the evening, a meal with drink, music and dancing. Visitors will often be made welcome at such celebrations.

Discos are common in cities and resorts. They range from sophisticated Athens nightspots to enthusiastic and unpredictable local arrangements which can be just as much fun. Most towns and even some large villages have cinemas, sometimes open-air, often showing foreign films with Greek subtitles.

Greek dancing is always popular

WEATHER AND WHEN TO GO

Greece is 'open' to visitors from about Easter to mid-October, although at either end of that period not all hotels and restaurants will be open. The best times to visit are May and September, when the sun is shining, the crowds fewer and the countryside at its best. Temperatures then average about 25°C, (hotter in the Peloponnese), but nights are cool and there may be a day or two of rain. Pack accordingly – shorts, T-shirts and light cotton

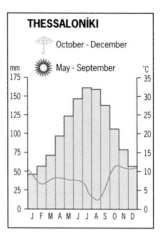

THESSALONÍKI

☂ October - December

☀ May - September

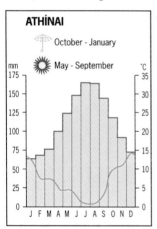

ATHÍNAI

☂ October - January

☀ May - September

items for the day (including cover-ups for visiting monasteries), with a sweater or jacket for the evenings. Greece is very informal.

Midsummer temperatures average more than 30°C. In August there have been several heatwaves in recent years, with temperatures nearing 40°C. In Athens this means intense

discomfort and an increase in air pollution. In mountain areas there is still a chance of rain, but in the south or near the coast you are unlikely to need to wrap up against rain or cold. Rainstorms are of the Mediterranean variety: intense but brief. Winters are mild. Average temperatures drop to 10-15°C (lower in the north), and snow or storms are likely in the mountains. But despite the unpredictable climate, this can still be a good time for a touring holiday, with classical sites deserted and many days of glorious sunshine.

HOW TO BE A LOCAL

It may seem that Greek men spend a great deal of time sitting in cafés, drinking coffee, playing cards and arguing. That is only a partial picture. Many work very hard, perhaps at two or three jobs, or making a tough living from the land. Fishermen will have been up most of the night, and during the summer season many people work for months on end with scarcely a day off. Nevertheless, the best way to get a glimpse of ordinary Greek life is to sit in a café for an hour, nursing a coffee. Ask for a *metrio* (medium), which has a little sugar to counteract the bitterness of the strong Greek coffee. *Sketo* is sugar-free, and *gliko* sweet. Greek coffee is served in tiny cups, and with a glass of water for cleansing the palate.

Eat in the tavernas where the locals eat. Watching a Greek family at a meal is a pleasure in itself, and you are sure to be in a place where food, service and value are all good.

Travel by bus, if only for a day out. Tickets are cheap, but sometimes need to be bought before boarding, often from a café or shop near the stop which acts as a ticket office. Buses are another excellent place for people-watching, and often provide a free introduction to ethnic music as you rattle along country roads with the radio playing at full blast.

Lose all track of time. Buses and ferries frequently do. Timetables are usually approximations, and while waiting for the bus to arrive you must be prepared to do as the Greeks do: sit, watch, and contemplate life... then rush in an elbowing crowd for the door when it appears.

Make the effort to master a few words of Greek. Even the most basic pleasantries such as 'please' and 'thank you' (see pages 124-5) will be very much appreciated, and you will probably find many a willing impromptu tutor, especially in country areas.

CHILDREN

The Greeks love children, making them welcome in hotels and tavernas, and tolerating crying babies, or the fractious behaviour of tired youngsters. In a friendly taverna you may even find that your child will be looked after by the staff, leaving you to enjoy a peaceful meal. Food should not be a problem. If children insist on nothing more adventurous than chips then these are available on almost every Greek menu, along with other plain and simple fare such as fish or perhaps burgers. Canned drinks are widely available. Greek ice-cream is good, and sticky desserts prove popular with young children.

Sea and sand are within easy reach of nearly all the most popular places. Special facilities for children are seldom provided, though there will be playgrounds and perhaps separate swimming pools in larger resorts and hotels. Children often play in large rowdy groups in the evening, in town and village squares throughout Greece, and visitors can easily join in.

You may think that children will not enjoy classical sites, but ancient theatres and other ruins can make wonderful giant playgrounds. Climbing to the back row, or play-acting on the stage, can provide memorable distractions and be a welcome release after travelling.

Relaxing is a way of life in Greece

Watching for lizards or insects and identifying wild flowers is another good pastime in such places. If you do not over-extend the stay, children and culture can be successfully combined.

TIGHT BUDGET

Greece is ideal for travellers on a budget, being one of the cheapest countries in Europe, but the following few tips can make it cheaper still.

● Most sites and public museums are free on one day of the week, almost always Sundays but with a few exceptions, so check.

● When eating out, watch where the locals eat, in particular priests and servicemen. Likely to be on a tight budget themselves, they can be relied on to find the best value for money.

● Snacks such as cheese (*tiropitakia*) or spinach (*spanakopites*) pies, widely available in towns, are cheap and filling.

● Perhaps contrary to your expectations, fish can be an expensive meal (see page 98). The most expensive salad is the ubiquitous Greek or country salad (*horiatiki*), with feta cheese and all the trimmings, so to save money choose a tomato (*domatosalata*) or tomato and cucumber salad (*angourodomata*).

● Retsina is the cheapest drink, but be sure to ask for a small bottle of a brand like Kourtaki, or you may get an up-market type at an up-market price.

● The Greek system of grading hotels is a better guide to price than to facilities. Some 'B' and even 'C' class hotels provide everything you need at half the cost of an 'A' class. Hostels are usually extremely basic, while 'rooms to rent' can offer the best value: often merely a spare bedroom, with shared use of the bathroom, but at a reasonable price. See also **Camping** (page 111).

● Greece has a good bus network, which is a very cheap means of transport. Hitch-hiking is common, but can be slow. Greek car insurance does not always cover additional passengers, so drivers may be reluctant to stop.

SPECIAL EVENTS

Processions mark many festivals

SPECIAL EVENTS

Almost every day in Greece – especially in summer – is a special event. There are hundreds of Orthodox Saints whose feast days are celebrated somewhere in the country, at churches bearing their name. As with a name day, there will be a church service in the morning, frequently early, and a communal meal with music and dancing in the evening. The exact turn of events depends on the stature of the Saint and the size of the community celebrating.

One thing to watch out for is the Greek fondness for celebrating on the eve of an event, the *paramoni*. Always be prepared to celebrate local events the night before!

The main events of the Greek year are as follows.

January
New Year's Day is celebrated, as is 6 January, the **Epiphany**, when it is a tradition for priests in seaside and lakeside locations to throw a cross into the water; local boys then compete to retrieve it.

February/March
Shrove Tuesday or *Mardi Gras* is not celebrated as widely in Greece as elsewhere in the world, though there are costume parties in Patraï, a tradition of hitting people on the head with plastic hammers in Athens, and widespread celebrations in Makedhonia.
Independence Day (25 March) commemorates the start of the revolt against Turkish domination.

April
Easter is the biggest single event in the Greek calendar. This movable feast coincides with the rest of the world's Easter only once every few years. Easter Sunday normally falls between mid-April and early May, so this is a wonderful time to visit Greece, coinciding with the arrival of warm weather and the opening of hotels and tavernas.
Easter rituals begin in the week leading up to Good Friday. Visit the local churches late in this week to see the glorious floral decorations. Children will often call on houses in the neighbourhood, distributing flowers and singing. On Good Friday evening, after a service, a magnificently decorated bier (to carry Christ's body) travels in a procession through the streets. Visitors need feel no

inhibitions about joining the walkers. In some places a bonfire follows, in which an effigy of Judas Iscariot is burned. Elsewhere this happens on Easter Sunday.

On Easter Saturday evening the main service takes place, culminating at midnight when all the lights are put out for a short time. After a pause, the priest lights a candle held by the nearest member of the congregation, who will in turn light candles held by other people, until the church glows with golden faces. The priest announces '*Christos Anesti*' (Christ is risen), the response being '*Alithos Anesti*' (He is risen indeed). The news is celebrated by the return of the lights and by fireworks in the streets. As the people walk home from church, they keep their candle flames lit, carrying them over the threshold to bring good fortune throughout the year. Many families eat *magaritsa*, the traditional Easter soup of rice, lemon and lamb offal.

Easter Sunday is a family day. A morning service is followed by a huge Sunday lunch, when the rest of the lamb is eaten. You may see a game in which Easter eggs, (hard-boiled eggs painted red) are knocked against each other to see who has the last uncracked egg. Other festivities may include a communal evening meal with traditional dancing.

May

May Day (1 May) is celebrated everywhere. Cities may have traditional workers' parades, while elsewhere this is a day for family picnics and flower-gathering. The flowers are plaited into wreaths and hung on doors until 24 June, the feast of St John the Reaper, when they are burned as summer is considered to have safely arrived.

Feast of Saints Konstantinos and Eleni (21 May) Fire-walking demonstrations take place in some Makedhonian villages.

August

Feast of the Assumption of the Blessed Virgin Mary (*Apokimisis tis Panagias*) (15 August). Greeks everywhere try to return to their home village for this important date, and ferries to the islands are often full. On the mainland you will find many hotels fully booked around this day, so it is not a good time to be travelling speculatively. However, if you are staying somewhere you may be able to attend a service at the local church or monastery, often followed by feasting, music and dancing.

October

Ohi Day (28 October) commemorates the day in 1940 when the Greek leader, General Metaxas, gave a one-word response, '*Ohi*' (No), to an ultimatum from Mussolini that his troops be allowed to pass through Greece.

December

Christmas and **New Year's Eve** wind down the Greek year, though they are less important to Greek people than Easter.

SPORT

Greek men, generally speaking, are sports-mad – after all, they invented the Olympic Games. However, most of them today are armchair sportsmen, preferring to watch football or basketball on TV in the local taverna – an interest seldom shared by their womenfolk.

Football is a national obsession, and you will probably find as much drama at a local game on a makeshift pitch as at a first-division match in Athens or Thessaloniki. The teams to watch here are Panathinaikos and AEK in Athens, and PAOK in Thessaloniki.

An interest in **basketball** has developed almost to the point of fanaticism in recent years, since the Greek team won the European Championship.

On the active side, watersports are common. Most larger resorts have **windsurfing** and

Watersports in Khalkidhiki

water-skiing facilities, with tuition. **Paragliding** is increasingly popular, and it is usually easy to hire water-scooters, pedaloes and boats. The clear Greek waters are ideal for **scuba-diving**, but restrictions apply because the seas still contain many antiquities and there have been thefts in the past. Use of a mask and snorkel is permitted, but full breathing apparatus is forbidden. On the mainland, scuba-diving is concentrated on the Khalkidhiki peninsula.

For information about **sailing**, contact the Greek Sailing Federation at Xenofondhos 15a, Athens (tel: 01–323–5560 or 01-323–6813). Also in Athens is the Hellenic Windsurfing Association, at Fil Fileninon 7 (tel: 01–323–0068 or 01-323–0330).

Greece is not famous for its **golf**, but there are courses in Glyfada on the outskirts of Athens (tel: 01–894–6820) and at Porto Carras in Khalkidhiki (tel: 0375-71381/71221).

Skiing is one of Greece's lesser-known recreations, but there are ski-lifts and facilities on Mount Olympos, in the Pindhos, at Metsovon, on Mount Pilion, in the Parnassos range and elsewhere. For full details, contact the Greek Skiing and Alpine Federation, Karayeorgi 7, Athens (tel: 01–323–4555).

Greece is wonderful for **walking**. If you plan to visit remote areas, or think you may need to stay at a mountain refuge, get information from the Greek Alpine Club, Eolou 68–70, Athens (tel: 01–321–2429).

Directory

This section (with the biscuit-coloured band) contains day-to-day information, including travel, health and documentation.

Contents

Arriving
By Air

There are scheduled flights to Athens from many countries, and the Greek national airline, Olympic Airways, covers most routes alongside other major airlines. Olympic also flies to Thessaloniki from some countries, and in summer charter flights are available to other mainland airports such as Kalamai (for the southern Peloponnese) and Preveza (for northern and western Greece). Domestic flights are operated by Olympic, and it is possible to make connections at Athens (and a few at Thessaloniki) for several provincial airports. Olympic uses the western terminal at Ellinikon International Airport in Athens while all other airlines use the eastern terminal; both are in the suburb of Glyfada, 10km southeast of the city centre. They are barely five minutes apart, but the shuttle service between them only operates hourly from 08.30–20.30hrs, otherwise take a taxi.

Taxis are also the quickest way into central Athens, but far from the cheapest. As with every major airport, taxi-drivers here include some rogues. The fare into Athens should be about 1,500 drachma, so agree this before setting off or insist that the meter is on. Check that the meter has a figure '1' illuminated. A figure '2' indicates a double fare, allowed only between midnight and 06.00, or for travel outside the city boundaries (which does not apply to the airport). It is not uncommon for fares of five or ten times the right amount to be demanded, and paid by unwary visitors.

An easy and much cheaper alternative is the blue and yellow Express Bus from the stop directly outside each terminal building. Separate buses operate to and from the two terminals every 15 minutes, direct to Platia Sindagma (Syntagma Square). There is no metro or train station near the airport.

Both terminals have banking and shopping facilities, although these are minimal. They are well served by car-hire companies, with small offices for major names such as Hertz, Avis and Budget.

By Sea

There are regular ferries to mainland Greece from the Italian ports of Ancona, Bari, Otranto and Brindisi. These go to either Igoumenitsa in northern Ipiros (Epirus), or Patrai (Patras) in the northern Peloponnese, sometimes to both, and sometimes with a stop at Kerkyra (Corfu). A service also runs from Trieste to Patrai.

There are many ferry services in and out of Piraeus, the port of Athens and one of the busiest in the Mediterranean. Some of the major international routes link Piraeus with Venice and Ancona in Italy, Kusadasi and

Izmir in Turkey, Limassol and Larnaca in Cyprus, Haifa in Israel, and Port Said and Alexandria in Egypt. Ferries also run between Piraeus and most of the major Greek islands.

Piraeus is a typical port, full of life – though some of it not the kind many visitors may wish to see. Its metro station links with central Athens, the most convenient stops being Monastiraki (for the Plaka), or Platia Omonia (Omonia Square). The service runs from 06.00 to 24.00hrs. The local bus, route 041, is not conveniently located and the Express Bus, route 19, runs every 30 minutes from Piraeus to the western and eastern air terminals but not to the city centre. A taxi from Piraeus to the centre should cost about 1,200 drachmae, but the warnings in the **By Air** section apply here, too.

Train travel may not be the fastest or the most flexible option, but it is an unbeatable way to relax and enjoy the scenery

By Road
The most popular route to
Greece from northern Europe
is through Italy and across the
Adriatic by ferry. The main
highway through the former
Yugoslavia has been closed for
some time, necessitating a
diversion to the east towards
Budapest and Belgrade. This is
the route favoured by coach
services, including members of
the Eurolines network which
covers most European
countries.

By Rail
A rail journey from northern
Europe to Athens takes roughly
three days. The price is almost
as much as a scheduled flight,
so there is little saving unless a
student or other discount
applies.

Entry Formalities
Citizens of the USA, Canada,
Australia, the European
Community and most non-EC
Europeans require only a valid
passport for entry to Greece,
allowing a stay of 90 days (60
days for New Zealand).
Extensions are possible by

applying to the *Ipiresia
Allodhapon* (Aliens' Bureau) in
most large Greek cities.

Camping
There are not as many official
campsites in Greece as in
some other countries, but
enough for touring visitors to
be fairly sure of finding one.
For a list, contact Association
Greek Camping, Solonos 102,
Athens 10680 (tel:
01–362–1560). Prices and
facilities vary, but if your needs
are basic the cost will be
remarkably low. An
International Camping Carnet is
useful, though not normally
requested. The Greek National
Tourist Organisation runs a
chain of sites, where standards
and prices are higher.
Unofficial camping is illegal,
though common in practice.
However, if you are asked to
move, do so politely: you are
breaking the law and the
possible consequences are
serious.
Lighting fires is unwise: there
have been terrible forest fires
in Greece in recent years, and
campfires are prohibited in
many places. Take great care.

Car Rental
Hire cars are available at
Athens airport and in most
cities, large towns and tourist
resorts. Rates are expensive.
Your own driving licence will
normally be adequate, whether
booking in the country or
abroad in advance, although in
theory an International Driving
Licence may be required.
Minimum age varies from 21 to
25, according to the hire
company.

DIRECTORY

The world is your oyster in Piraeus

It is best to hire from a recognised company: rates may be higher but the car will be safer. Rental cars in holiday areas are heavily used, and smaller companies with small fleets tend to run them through the season with minimal servicing. This applies even more to motorbike or moped hire.

The insurance cover insisted on by law and included in standard agreements is generally not adequate should there be a serious accident. Always check what cover you have, and whether additional cover is available. It is advisable to add Collision Damage Waiver (CDW) insurance, at a small extra cost: rental companies will probably try to sell you this anyway. It gives you full insurance cover, no matter who was responsible for any accident.

Crime

Greece is one of the safest countries in Europe, and it is very rare for a visitor to fall victim to a crime. In rural areas, especially, the local people would be horrified at the thought. Other tourists are not necessarily as honest, though, so you should look after money and valuables. It is probably wise not to offer lifts.

Customs Regulations

The normal EC regulations apply. Ordinary travellers will be unlikely to exceed the new, more generous EC duty-paid allowances, but if in doubt, check before departure.

Cats and dogs require health and rabies inoculation certificates, from a veterinary authority in the country of origin, dated not less than six days or more than 12 months (cats six months) from the date of arrival.

Antiquities and works of art can be imported, but must be declared and the value stated if they are to be exported again. It is forbidden to export antiquities and works of art found in Greece. The allowances for exporting other goods vary with the destination so check this before departure.

Disabled Visitors

Greece can be difficult for disabled visitors. Hotel and other facilities lag behind the times. Assume nothing, and check everything in advance. Useful organisations to contact in the country include Lavinia Tours, Egnatia 101, Thessaloniki 54110, and the archaically named but helpful National Association of Rehabilitation for the Handicapped, Odhos Hassias, Nea Liossia, KA 1322 Athens.

Driving

Driving in Greece can be a great joy. Many roads are quiet, with views of spectacular scenery. A car offers access to much more of the country, including places that are virtually inaccessible by public transport.

Nevertheless, Greece has the worst road safety record in Europe, with an average of seven deaths per day on the roads. Care must therefore be taken. Driving is on the right, but be prepared for locals using the centre of the road, especially when coming round corners.

Speed limits, though often ignored, are 50kph (31mph) in built-up areas, 80kph (49mph) outside built-up areas and 100kph (62mph) on dual carriageways. Road signs are poor, and a good map is essential. Signposts for through-routes in towns and cities are notably lacking, and understanding Greek directions can be a problem. Signs to archaeological sites and villages can frequently be seen from one side only. A knowledge of the Greek alphabet is vital: main roads are usually signposted in both Greek and Roman characters, but side-roads often carry only Greek names.

Seat belts must be worn where fitted, and drivers can be fined for not carrying a warning triangle, a fire extinguisher and a first-aid kit. Tolls apply on motorways, but Greek motorways can be rather unpredictable: four lanes can become two without warning, and slow-moving farm vehicles are often found. In rural areas a smooth road can suddenly become a dirt track. Herds of animals are a common hazard. Any accident causing bodily injury must be reported to the police, and you must stop and give assistance or you may face a jail sentence. Accidents causing material damage only should still be reported to the police as a precaution.

Drinking and driving is a serious offence in Greece, with a prison sentence as a possible penalty. The best advice is not to drink any alcohol if you are driving.

Petrol

Unleaded petrol is quite widely available, and petrol stations exist in all but the tiniest of villages. They are normally open seven days a week, from about 08.00hrs until early evening, with an afternoon break. Some close on Sundays. Finding petrol is not a problem, but paying for it can be. Petrol is expensive, and few garages take credit cards. 'Super' is equivalent to high-octane 4-star (96-98 octane) and 'regular' equivalent to 2-star (91-92 octane). A useful word is *yemiste*, full.

See also **Arriving** (page 111) and **Car Rental** (pages 111-12).

Electricity
Voltage is 220 AC. Most normal electrical gadgets such as hairdriers will work, although visitors from some countries will need a converter while others will require an adaptor for the European round two-pin sockets used in Greece. There are occasional power cuts so a torch is useful.

Embassies and Consulates
Australia
Mesoghion 15, Athens (tel: 01–775–7650/4)
Canada
G.Gennadiou 4, Athens (tel: 01–723–9510/9)
Ireland
Vass. Konstantinou 7, Athens

An unmistakably Greek scene

(tel: 01–723–2771/2)
New Zealand
Semitelou 9, Athens (tel: 01–771–0112)
United Kingdom
Ploutarchou 1, Athens (tel: 01–723–6211/9)
Venizelou 8, Thessaloniki (tel: 031–278006)
USA
Vass. Sophias 91, Athens (tel: 01–721–2951/9, 01–721–8400/1)
Nikis 59, Thessaloniki (tel: 031–266121)

Emergency Telephone Numbers
In Athens, for a medical emergency call 166, or 171 for the Tourist Police. Elsewhere dial 166 for an ambulance or 100 (*ekato*), which connects you to the branch of the police known as the *Ekato*, who deal not only with crime but also with fire and medical emergencies.

Health
No inoculations are required, but it is a wise precaution to have a typhoid-cholera booster and ensure that you are up to date with tetanus and polio jabs. Water is safe to drink, but many people prefer bottled water. Health centres exist in most towns, and are well signposted in both Greek and English. Opening hours are usually 08.00–12.00hrs only. State hospitals offer free medical attention to EC citizens for emergencies, although 'free' can mean paying first and claiming a refund later. Should anything happen requiring lengthy attention, seek private treatment, which is superior to

Athens: the Memorial to the Unknown Soldier, on Syntagma Square

basic state care. Health insurance providing adequate cover is obviously essential. There will be doctors in most large villages: like pharmacists, they are highly trained, usually speak English and (like most Greek people) will do their best to help you.

Sunburn is a common problem: cooling breezes can be deceptive and the Greek sun is fierce. Use protection for the first few days, and acclimatise yourself gradually, easing off only if you are sure your skin can take more exposure. Be especially careful with children, ensuring they use a sun-block cream and preferably wear a hat too. Take salt with food and drink plenty of fluids.

When swimming, watch out for sea urchins and jellyfish. The former are common in rocky areas, so wear light shoes. Should one of the black spines pierce your skin, it must be removed. Ask local people or a pharmacist for help. Jellyfish are less common and not all are poisonous, but if you are stung painfully, a pharmacist will be able to suggest a remedy. See also **Pharmacies**, page 118.

Holidays

Sites and museums are closed on the public holidays of 1 January, 25 March (except Navplion's Palamidi Fortress), Good Friday until noon, Easter Sunday, 1 May, 25 and 26 December. In addition there are half-holidays, when weekend opening hours apply, on 6 January, the first Monday in Lent, Easter Saturday, Easter Monday, Whit Sunday, 15 August and 28 October.

Shops and some restaurants close on public holidays, and on the afternoon before and the morning after a religious holiday. This is less likely to be observed in tourist areas, and wherever you are, some tavernas will be open. Take care in rural areas if you need supplies and a holiday is imminent.

Lost Property

If you lose something there is a strong chance it will still be waiting for you if you know where you lost it. The vast majority of Greeks are extremely honest. If you cannot

The freshest of fresh produce at a country market

recall where it went missing, report it to the hotel management or the Tourist Police.

Media

Television
Greece has two national television channels, ET1 and ET2. Both broadcast a number of American TV programmes and films with Greek subtitles. There are also an increasing number of satellite channels.

Radio
Greek airwaves are full of stations national, international and local, and Greek music is never far away. The two state channels are known as ERT1 and ERT2, though the former is divided up into three programmes on different frequencies. There are early morning news summaries in English, German, Arabic and French at 07.40hrs daily on 728KHz. English news bulletins are also broadcast daily at 14.00hrs and 21.00hrs on ERT2 (98KHz).

The BBC World Service can be picked up on various frequencies: in Athens try 9.41, 12.09 or 15.07MHz. In the Athens area the American Forces Radio Service broadcasts on 1484 and 1594KHz.

Magazines and Newspapers
In Athens most major European newspapers are widely available on the evening of the day of publication or the following morning. American newspapers and international magazines are also available, though at high prices. Outside Athens availability is obviously better in tourist areas, and in summer.

There are several English-language publications in Greece, such as the daily (except Monday) *Athens News*, the *Greek Weekly News*, the monthly *Athenian* and *30 Days: Greece This Month*. These are easily found in Athens and popular tourist areas, less so elsewhere. They carry information on local events and temporary exhibitions.

Money Matters

The Greek currency is the drachma. You may find a few 1- and 2-drachma coins, but these are of such low value that change is normally given to the nearest 5 drachma. There are also coins for 10, 20, 50 and 100 drachma, with notes for 50, 100, 500, 1,000 and 5,000.

A Greek idiosyncrasy is that no one ever seems to have any change, and you are constantly expected to produce the exact amount for any transaction. . Visitors may take up to 100,000 drachma into the country and take 20,000 drachma out. It is a good idea to have some small-denomination notes when you arrive. Travellers' cheques to any amount can be imported and exported, but cash of over £600 for EC citizens (£300 non-EC) should be declared at Customs if you want to take it out again.

Travellers' cheques can be changed at most banks, hotels and post offices, on production of a passport, and in some shops and restaurants in tourist areas, though sometimes with a less favourable rate of exchange. Post offices generally charge a lower commission than banks or tourist exchanges. Look for the yellow English-language 'EXCHANGE' sign. Banks and post offices are generally open from 08.00 or 08.30hrs to 14.00hrs on weekdays only. Eurocheques are widely accepted in banks, but not necessarily elsewhere, while credit cards are increasingly accepted in the more expensive hotels, shops and restaurants in popular areas. Do not assume, however, that you need only 'plastic' money. In Greece it is normal to settle even large transactions in cash, so do not be caught out. 'No cheques' is a common sign, even in some Athens hotels.

Opening Times

(See **Holidays**, page 115, for days when establishments of all kinds will be closed.)

Banks

See **Money Matters**, above.

Museums and Sites

Opening hours issued by official sources will frequently disagree with those shown at a site or museum. Those displayed at the place itself are usually the ones given in this book, but these may change without notice according to availability of local staff. The book gives summer opening hours, which are slightly longer than winter hours (the summer season runs from 1 April to 31 October).

The only thing it is safe to assume about Greek opening hours is that it is not safe to assume anything. If you are setting out on a special journey, try to check current opening hours before you go.

Shops

Shops traditionally open from 08.00 to 13.00hrs, when they close for the afternoon. They reopen from about 17.00 to 20.00hrs, though some supermarkets and shops catering to visitors stay open much later. Opening and closing times may vary by an hour or so. In many areas – and especially in tourist resorts in the summer season – there has recently been an increasing tendency for shops to abandon the mid-day break, remaining open all day. Shops generally close on Sundays, except in tourist areas.

Pharmacies

Ask for the *farmakio* or look for the green-cross sign. Greek pharmacists have medical training and are often multilingual. They can give advice and prescriptions for common ailments. If you need prescription drugs, remember to take the exact details with you from home in case extra supplies are needed. Note that codeine, widely available elsewhere, is banned in Greece and visitors have been fined for carrying it.

Pharmacies open during normal shop hours, but are closed on Saturdays and Sundays. A 24-hour rota system operates outside normal hours, and each shop will post details of the nearest open pharmacy (but, of course, the notice will be in Greek).

Places of Worship

You can scarcely walk for five minutes in any direction without encountering a Greek Orthodox church. Many are kept open, but those with precious icons or other valuables may be locked, in which case the key will be available from a keyholder nearby. Ask at the nearest shop or café.

The Greek landscape is dotted with churches and chapels, many of the tiny remote ones holding a service only once a year, on its own Saint's feast day. Sunday services start early, at about 07.30 or 08.00hrs, and last for several hours. Many people call in for a while, then leave again, rather than stay for the whole service. Visitors may attend, provided they dress decently and behave discreetly.

There are other religious denominations, but their importance is indicated by the fact that almost 97 per cent of Greeks are Greek Orthodox. In Athens there is the Roman Catholic church of Ayios Dionysios on Omirou, the Anglican church of Ayios Pavlos at Philhellinon 29 and the nearby Russian Orthodox church of Ayios Nikodimos. There are also two Protestant churches on Sina: the German Evangelical Christos Kirche and the American interdenominational church of St Andrew.

Outside Athens you are unlikely to find non-Orthodox services.

Police

The affairs of visitors are looked after by the Tourist Police, a separate branch of the police force. They make regular checks on facilities and charges in hotels and restaurants. Usually fluent in at least one foreign language, they should be your first call if you run into trouble, whether over a dispute with a taxi-driver or in the unlikely event of a serious crime.

See also **Emergency Telephone Numbers**, page 114.

Post Office

These are distinguished by a yellow 'OTE' sign. Most communities from large villages upwards have a post office. Many of them will cash travellers' cheques and exchange currency: look for the 'EXCHANGE' sign. They are normally open during morning shop hours only, but a post office in each large city will also be open on Saturday mornings. Queues can be long and slow, as counters offer a range of services. If you only want stamps (*grammatosima*) for postcards, or for letters up to 20gm, try kiosks or shops selling postcards. Parcels for posting must be inspected by the post office clerk before sealing.

Post-boxes are small yellow boxes, with no distinguishing features unless you find one with two slots, in which case *Exoteriko* is for overseas mail.

Greeks never seem to be in a hurry

Air-mail letters usually take three to six days to reach the rest of Europe, five to eight days for North America, slightly longer for Australasia. Postcards take longer.

Public Transport

Buses

Greek buses are the best way to travel, being cheap and reasonably regular. See **How to Be a Local**, page 104, for more information. Note that smoking is banned for passengers, and the playing of loud music seems compulsory for drivers. GNTO offices can provide timetables of services from Athens. A route map is available from the EOT in Athens.

Buses and trolleys in Athens display their number and destination at the front. A flat-fare ticket must be bought before boarding, at the ticket booths near most stops or from news kiosks. Stamp your ticket in the machine just inside the bus door.

DIRECTORY

Ferries

See **Arriving**, page 110, for boats to Greece. Many mainland towns have services to certain islands, the main port being Piraeus in Athens. If you are moving on from the mainland, bear in mind that there are several different harbours in Piraeus, quite some distance apart, and it is important to establish which one your boat will be leaving from. Obtain an up-to-date timetable from the Greek National Tourist Organisation.

Trains

Greek trains are even cheaper than buses, but usually slower, and the network is restricted. Going northwest from Athens, for example, the line stops at Kalabaka for Meteora, and you will have to take a bus to travel further west to Ipiros or north to the Pindhos. Likewise, Kalamai is the most southerly place in the Peloponnese that can be reached by train. Timetables can be obtained from GNTO offices but, as with ferries, these are often subject to late changes.

Taxis

Taxis are cheap by comparison with other countries, and it is common to book them for much longer journeys than you might contemplate elsewhere. Most are metered, but see **Arriving** for possible problems of overcharging. Drivers are allowed to stop to pick up other passengers going in the same direction,provided the first passenger has no objection. Because Greeks use taxis constantly, it can be hard to find one. In Athens you could probably walk to your destination before managing to flag one down, so book ahead if the journey is important. Elsewhere the number of taxi licences is limited according to the perceived needs of the local population. This means that in popular tourist resorts in summer there are likely to be too few taxis available.

The Athens Metro

Although there is only one metro line, it runs from the

Piraeus – the gateway to Greek islands near and far

'Rooms' are often excellent value

northern suburb of Kifissia, where there are campsites and hotels, through central Athens and out to Piraeus in the south. Convenient central stops include Omonia and Monastiraki for the Plaka and the Akropolis. The service runs every 15 minutes, from 05.00 to 24.00hrs. Not all trains run the full length of the line, so check the destination board. Tickets must be bought before travelling, from machines or ticket offices at the station.

Senior Citizens

The midsummer Greek heat is fierce, and if a sudden heatwave strikes there are often reports of elderly people succumbing to sunstroke. Consider travelling before July or after mid-September, when the weather will be hot but not deadly.

If you like to sit and watch the world go by, you have a great deal in common with the senior citizens of Greece... and the ideal place in which to do it. If you do not wish to drive, there are numerous coach trips from resort areas taking in classical sites. For the active, there are many companies offering walking holidays to Greece. The mainland offers few opportunities for cheap, long-stay holidays out of season. Hotels tend to close then.

Student and Youth Travel

There are only a handful of Youth Hostels on the mainland, but they are well situated for the main areas of interest. There are three in Athens and one each in Thessaloniki, Delfi, Navplion, Olimbia, Mikinai, Patrai and Litokhoron. They are cheap and basic, and you need an international youth hostel card. These can be bought on arrival or in advance from the Greek Association of Youth Hostels, Dragatsaniou 4, Athens (tel: 01–323–4107). There are also YMCA and YWCA hostels in Athens and Thessaloniki. An International Student Identity Card can provide travel discounts and cheap entry to museums and classical sites.

Telephones

The easiest way to make a call is to go to almost any street-corner kiosk or shop, pick up the metered telephone and dial. Metered telephones like this are so commonplace that they usually warrant no special sign. You pay according to the meter reading when you have finished. This saves having to find a vast number of 10-, 20- and 50-drachma coins if you are calling abroad, these being the only ones accepted by pay-phones (an orange stripe indicates an international telephone). Direct-dial telephones are fairly common in good hotels, but charges are much higher than on metered telephones.

In many towns there are metered telephones in branches of the OTE (post office). These are sometimes in the main post office, sometimes in a separate building, and again you pay at the end of the call. Telephones may be available at times other than normal opening hours. Cheap-rate times for calls within Greece are 15.00–17.00hrs, 21.00–08.00hrs and at weekends. For international calls from the Greek mainland, a small discount applies from 22.00 to 08.00hrs. Connections for international calls are surprisingly good, though it is important to dial slowly. Dialling codes from Greece are:

Australia	0061
Canada and the USA	001
New Zealand	0064
UK and Ireland	0044
International Operator	161

You should then omit the initial zero of the area code you are dialling.

To call Greece from abroad, use the appropriate international code for Greece then the number, omitting the initial zero of the area code. In this book, local area codes are included in all telephone numbers except in the **Athens** section, where all numbers should be prefixed by 01 when dialled from outside the city.

Time

Greek time is two hours ahead of British time, one hour ahead of the rest of Western Europe, seven hours ahead of US and Canada Eastern Standard Time, ten hours ahead of Pacific Standard Time, and eight hours behind Australian New South Wales time.

From 1993, the date for changing the clocks in spring and autumn is the same in all EC countries. However, the beginning and end of Greek Summer Time may not coincide with the time change in other countries such as the USA. Do watch out for this if travelling at those times, especially in spring, when ferries and flights could be missed.

Dial 141 for a recorded time message in Greek.

Tipping

In restaurants service is included but it is normal to leave on the table any small change after paying the bill. Some people regard 100-drachma notes as small change. If you are very pleased with the service, a tip of a few hundred drachma would not go amiss. A small note also rewards the wine waiter or the person who clears the table.

In hotels you will seldom be pressured into tipping but a small gratuity to the porter or the barman of 10 per cent or a 100-drachma note will be welcomed. For chambermaids, 100 drachma per day left at the end of the stay would be generous. For taxi-drivers, 'keep the change' is the usual practice.

Toilets

Public toilets in Greece are few and far between, and those that do exist are probably better avoided. Finding a friendly taverna is the best option, but standards still vary enormously. What must be remembered is that Greek plumbing pipes have probably not improved in the last 2,000 years. They are of a small non-standard size, so easily become blocked if toilet paper is flushed down them. Only in the latest modern hotels is this usually an exception, and even here you should check first. In bathrooms and toilets there will be a waste bin for the disposal of toilet paper and sanitary towels. It may seem unhygienic, but is better than a blocked pipe flooding the room when you try to flush the toilet.

Tourist Offices

The Greek National Tourist Organisation (GNTO) has offices in:

Australia

51-7 Pitt Street, Sydney, NSW 2000 (tel: 02–241–1663)

Canada

1300 Bay Street, Main Level, Toronto, Ontario M5R 3K8 (tel: 416–968–2220)
1223 Rue de la Montagne, Montreal, Quebec H3G 1Z2 (tel: 514–871–1535)

United Kingdom

4 Conduit Street, London W1R 0DJ (tel: 071–734–5997)

United States of America

645 Fifth Avenue, New York, NY 10022 (tel: 212–421–5777)
168 North Michigan Avenue, Chicago IL 60601 (tel: 312–728–1084)
611 West 6th St, Suite 1998, Los Angeles, CA 90017 (tel: 213–626–6696)

There are also offices in most large towns and cities in Greece, the principal office for Athens being inside the National Bank building in Platia Sindagma though the address is Karayeorgi Servias 2 (tel: 01–322–2545).

The priest (papas) is revered, but not remote from everyday life

LANGUAGE

LANGUAGE

Unless you know the Greek script, a vocabulary will not be of very much use. But it is helpful to know the alphabet, so that you can find your way around; and the following few transliterated basic words and phrases will help too. (See also **Food and Drink** page 97–9).

Alphabet

Alpha	Aα	short a, as in hat
Beta	Bβ	v sound
Gamma	Γγ	guttural g sound
Delta	Δδ	hard th, as in father
Epsilon	Eε	short e
Zita	Zζ	z sound
Eta	Ηη	long e, as in feet
Theta	Θθ	soft th, as in think
Iota	Iι	short i, as in hit
Kappa	Κκ	k sound
Lambda	Λλ	l sound
Mu	Μμ	m sound
Nu	Νν	n sound
Xi	Ξξ	x or ks sound
Omicron	Οο	short o, as in pot
Pi	Ππ	p sound
Rho	Ρρ	r sound
Sigma	Σσ	s sound
Taf	Ττ	t sound
Ipsilon	Υυ	another ee sound, or y as in funny
Phi	Φφ	f sound
Chi	Χχ	guttural ch, as in loch
Psi	Ψψ	ps, as in chops
Omega	Ωω	long o, as in bone

Numbers

1	éna
2	dio
3	tria
4	téssera
5	pénde
6	éxi
7	eptá
8	októ
9	ennía
10	déka
11	éndeka
12	dódeka
13	dekatría
14	dekatéssera
15	dekapénde
16	dekaéxi
17	dekaeptá
18	dekaokto
19	dekaennía
20	ikosi
30	triánda
40	saránda
50	peninda
100	ekató
101	ekaton éna
1000	chília

Basic vocabulary

good morning	kaliméra
good evening	kalispéra
goodnight	kaliníkta
goodbye	chérete
hello	yásou
thank you	efharistó
please/you're welcome	parakaló
yes	ne
no	óchi
where is...?	poo íne?
how much is...?	póso káni?
I would like	tha íthela
do you speak English?	milate anglM-ÍM-:?

I would like	tha íthela
do you speak English?	milate angliká?
I don't speak Greek	then miló elliniká

Places

street	ódos
square	platía
restaurant	estiatório
hotel	xenodochío
room	domátio
post office	tachithromío
police	astinomía
pharmacy	farmakío
doctor	iatrós
bank	trápeza
hospital	nosokomío
café	kafeneion

Travelling

car	aftokínito
bus	leoforío
train	tréno
boat	karávi
garage	garáz
airport	aerodrómio
ticket	isitírio

Food and drink

food	fagitó
bread	psomí
water	neró
wine	krasí
beer	bíra
coffee	kafé

Fish

lobster	astakós
squid	kalamarákia
octopus	oktapóthi
red mullet	barboúnia
whitebait	marídes

Meat/poultry

lamb	arnáki
chicken	kotópoulo
meat balls	kefthédes
meat on a skewer	souvlákia

Vegetables

spinach	spanáki
courgette	kolokithia
beans	fasólia

Salads and starters

olives	eliés
yoghurt and cucumber dip	tzatsiki
tomato and cucumber salad	angour domata
stuffed vine leaves	dolmadakia
'Greek' salad with cheese	horiatiki

A Note on Transliteration

The Greek alphabet cannot be translated into other languages in a straightforward manner. This means that romanised spellings of Greek words can vary. In place-name headings, and in the Index, this book uses the transliterations that correspond to AA maps. More familiar anglicised spellings (given in brackets in the headings) are sometimes used in the text. This inevitably leads to inconsistencies when compared to other books, leaflets and road signs: Nafplion, Navplion, Nauplion, Náfplio, Navplio and Nauplio are all the same town. However, the differences are seldom so great as to make a name unrecognisable.

Similarly there may be differing translations of the names of museums and other places of interest, so that what one source interprets as 'Historical and Ethnological Museum' may elsewhere be termed 'National Historical Museum'. To avoid confusion, place-name headings (for example in the Athens section) give the name in romanised Greek, followed by the most usual English translation in brackets.

INDEX

INDEX/ACKNOWLEDGEMENTS

Country Distinguishing Signs

On several maps, international distinguishing signs have been used to indicate the location of the countries that surround Greece. Thus:

(AL) = Albania   (BG) = Bulgaria   (TR) = Turkey

Acknowledgements

The Automobile Association wishes to thank the following photographers, libraries and organisations for their assistance in the preparation of this book.

Richard Surman was commissioned to take all the photographs (© AA Photo Library) except for:

J ALLAN CASH PHOTOLIBRARY *108* Pallini Beach, Khalkidhiki

MIKE GERRARD *4* Guard, *13* Market at Komotini, *46* Folk Museum, *49* Antique shop, *97* Peppers, *115* Guard

TERRY HARRIS *106* Celebration

NATURE PHOTOGRAPHERS LTD *14* Cistus (A J Cleave), *91* White Stork (P R Sterry), *96* Common Tree Frog (P R Sterry)

SPECTRUM COLOUR LIBRARY *Cover* Parthenon, *19* Mule, *72* Harbour, Paleo Epidhavros

TIM LARSEN –COLLINGE (© AA Photo Library) *102* Greek dancing, *105* old man, *114* old lady in church doorway, *119* Greek men on doorstep

The Automobile Association would also like to thank the **National Tourist Organisation of Greece** for their help, and the **Automobile and Touring Club of Greece** (ELPA) for their assistance in checking details in the Directory.

Series adviser : Christopher Catling   Verifier : David Hancock
Copy editor   : Julia Brittain   Indexer : Marie Lorimer